TANTRA

the Play of Awakening

D1203053

TANTRA

the Play of Awakening

SHAMBHAVI SARASVATI

JAYA KULA PRESS

4110 SE Hawthorne Blvd. #106
Portland, Oregon 97214
jayakula.org

Cover and interior design and layout:
Cecilia Sorochin / SoroDesign

Library of Congress Control Number: 2012937052
Sarasvati, Shambhavi
Tantra: the play of awakening
ISBN-13:
978-0-9841634-2-7
10: 0-9841634-2-5

Printed in the United States of America on acid-free paper.

For everyone, all

CONTENTS

LET'S GO

THIS BOOK IS a tour guide, a map and a friend for anyone on a conscious path of spiritual awakening. It wants to support you in your efforts to discover the wisdom inherent in Reality, to warn you of possible detours, to comfort, encourage, prod and make you laugh.

The teachings you'll encounter here are loosely organized. Feel free to skip around, meander, double back or read straight through. The final section is titled "Heart Advice," but in truth, the entire book is composed of teachings I received with my heart and am sharing with you from the heart—the heart of a practitioner, of a disciple and, more recently, a teacher.

In the direct realization traditions, such as Kashmir Shaivism and Dzogchen, we say: *Everything is fine.* Life is not a problem. We understand that whatever happens is Reality, aka God, expressing itself. Or as is said by the Dzogchen masters: *Everything is self-perfected from the beginning.*

If everything is fine, why bother teaching, or writing books?

Teaching is not fixing a problem. A plant taking in water is not fixing something. It is just being a plant. Teaching is also an aspect of nature, as is studenting. There is an ongoing teaching aspect that is part of the natural expression of life moving toward Self-recognition, or realization. Teaching, teacher and student are one natural, co-arising technology for delighting in the experience of waking up.

My root Guru, Anandamayi Ma, exhorted everyone to do spiritual practice. She urged people to turn their lives and activities toward Self-realization in whatever way they could. But there was no sense of personal urgency attached. She had total confidence in life. Her exhortations were just what was naturally happening—part of the expressive play of Reality. Nothing more or less.

On one level, I feel constant wonder that traditions, teachers and practices, such as those from which I have benefitted, exist at all. I want to share my wonder, and what I have learned, with you. I'd like you to deepen your practice, whatever it is. I want you to realize more of your nature and experience greater spaciousness, sensitivity and expressivity in your life as I have.

On another level, these affects and desires are all the same impulse of an aware, awake Reality accomplishing the revelation of itself to itself. It is all playfulness. I find it impossible at this stage to take writing, or teaching or even my own lingering earnestness too seriously. My students will confirm that I regularly break out into giggles while giving satsang and other teachings. That we show up and play together like this is wondrous, delightful and hilarious.

My previous book, *Pilgrims to Openness*, presented an overview of the tradition of direct realization Tantra (Kashmir Shaivism) and practical View teachings, many of them about how everyday life functions as spiritual practice. (So read it, if you haven't already! ☺)

View teachings help you to understand the larger context in which your practice is occurring. You learn about Reality from the perspective of those who have already realized. *That* Reality is more expansive than what you are likely experiencing right now.

View teachings also convey *how* to do spiritual practice and how to correctly orient yourself to your practice by understanding why you are doing it and what attitude to adopt as you do your practice.

For instance, people are often instructed to watch their breath. This instruction is commonly understood to be "meditation." Even when I specifically point out that I am *not* giving an instruction to watch the breath, some people slip into this behavior over time.

In my tradition, a beginning instruction would more likely be to *feel* the breath and to lose the watcher. This is a profoundly different instruction. Students have to know that it is important and why. When View teachings are given correctly and students are not too distracted to listen and absorb them, this kind of "slippage" does not occur.

View teachings are not theories. They are not simple information, or academic philosophy. View teachings are transmission teachings given by a person who has practiced, usually for a long time, and has realized the fruit of practice.

By receiving View teachings, you are already beginning to discover your real nature in a direct way. The alchemy that exists between you and the teacher causes you to have *an actual, embodied experience* of your own essence nature. This discovery, however fleeting, acts as a beacon. You can see where you are going and head more directly for that. Reading is different from hearing the teachings in the presence of the teacher, but it is still a useful practice.

This book is a collection of View teachings. It addresses many of the nitty gritty circumstances that arise when you are doing some kind of practice, most specifically in direct realization traditions. However, because all aspirants to Self-understanding eventually encounter similar circumstances, I think this book can be useful to anyone in any tradition. I know that I have received useful teachings from Buddhist, Christian, Daoist and other teachers.

Before we go any further, though, you and I have some cutting to do. We have to cut away a few powerful cultural dogmas about Self-realization, spirituality and Tantra.

Ready?

Let go.

CUTTING THROUGH

Even one moment of cutting-through clarity, during which your real nature stands revealed, can set you irrevocably on the path.

WHAT IS DIRECT REALIZATION TANTRA?

DIRECT REALIZATION TANTRA is what I call the North Indian tradition of Kashmir Shaivism. Kashmir Shaivism is a term invented by scholars. This doesn't make it wrong or bad, but it is not exactly user-friendly. And it doesn't tell you much other than that it comes from Kashmir and has something to do with Lord Shiva. On the other hand, having a direct experience of your own enlightened nature lies at the very heart of the tradition, at the heart of all the practices and at the heart of the relationship of teacher and student.

"Direct" means that the teacher reintroduces the student to her real nature. We call this processes of reintroduction "transmission." Transmission is not a description or a concept. The introduction is an actual experience that the student can recognize and return to over and over again until it becomes the student's base state.

"Realization" means that the student applies the methods in order to continuously remember and be in the state of the transmission. You could say that the student is being in the state of the teacher, or that the student is remembering and taking refuge in her own enlightened nature. These are the same because the enlightened state of the teacher and of the student are the same.

"Tantra" means, among other things, continuity. So direct realization Tantra means the practice and tradition of receiving the naturally arising transmission from the teacher and working to consciously and continuously embody *that*: your real nature, aka the realized Self.

The tradition of direct realization Tantra, or Kashmir Shaivism, is a synthesis of several Tantrik lineages that flourished during the fifth to eleventh centuries. The older name for this synthesis is *Trika*.

Abhinavagupta, the Tantrik siddha and scholar who is credited with birthing the synthetic tradition we are most familiar with today, wrote that Trika means Shiva, Shakti and their unison (Dhar 70).

Shiva is the personification of feeling-consciousness. Shakti is the personification of creative power, or energy. Shiva and Shakti are always united just as fire comprises light indissolubly united with heat. They are one, unbroken reality. In this book, I refer to the one continuous Reality composed of consciousness and energy as Shiva nature, or simply as the Self. Those who do Tantrik practice discover that everything is *that*.

While Shiva nature is one and continuous, it has the power, or Shakti, to create infinite experiences of diversity. Shiva nature's very life process is to manifest these experiences and to enjoy them. This is why the View of direct realization Tantra is properly called "*bhedabheda*" in Sanskrit, or "dualnondual." The livingness of Shiva nature includes everything: experiences of both duality (diversity) and nonduality (oneness).

In some Indian and other religious traditions, the manifest world of you, me, car and crow is viewed as either a dangerous illusion, degraded or both. Human senses and desires are viewed as problems. People in those traditions are taught that the ultimate goal of spiritual life is to transcend being human.

Direct realization Tantra teaches that being human is not a problem. Everything is Shiva nature. This manifest life of you, me, birds, trucks and toasters is the ornament, the theater or the glamour of Shiva nature. Glamour means both the glamorousness and the wondrous magic of Lord Shiva. Once we disentangle ourselves from the experience of suffering, we can enjoy ordinary life from an expanded and fresh perspective. We come to know directly that everything is the Self with Self playing all of the roles for her own delight. Since there is nothing here but Shiva nature, there is nothing to escape other than our limited experience of Reality.

Through the practice of direct realization Tantra, we want to emerge from our limited experience and come to embody the full glory of the Self. We realize that we *are* this pervasive consciousness and energy. We rest contentedly in our own nature and enjoy our own infinite display.

Sitting behind the experiences we call duality and nonduality is simple livingness. Once we reach a certain stage of Self-awareness, concepts such as duality and nonduality become unimportant and inadequate. We are just being livingness, immersed in livingness—our own nature—and enjoying that.

SPIRITUAL NOURISHMENT

It's so simple! A student exclaimed.

She was talking about the cosmos.

Once you begin to get it that the world is a continuity, you start to get that the processes that run the cosmos also are continuous and simple.

For instance, there is only one longing—the longing for Self-realization. This longing gets expressed differently depending on a person's degree of awareness. You may seek out a donut, a dollar or a dharma teacher, but these activities are all propelled by the same natural and inevitable force of longing to realize your nature.

A person who craves sweets longs to discover the nourishing, sweet essence of all existence. A person who craves financial security is longing for the refuge of his true home in the Self. A person who longs for a dharma teacher is beginning to wake up to the real destination toward which longing is leading her.

This is easy to recognize if you take a moment to tap into the feeling of longing. All longing feels the same. There are only varying intensities and objects to which longing attaches. Try it.

The entire cosmos functions just like this. The same processes are at work at every level from the most subtle to the most gross. The only distinction is the degree of awareness with which these processes are expressed.

So, let's consider digestion.

From a Tantrik perspective, the digestion of food, emotions, situations and wisdom exist along a continuum. They're all part of one world process: digestion. There is no radical difference between digesting a meal, digesting a difficult moment in a friendship and digesting spiritual teachings.

If we are eating efficiently—if our gross and subtle channels are open and functioning well—we extract a quantity of nourishment from either a meal, or a life change. What is not nourishing, we excrete. What we cannot digest or excrete makes us ill. People with more efficient, subtle and aware digestion can extract more nourishment from their food and from life in general. If we are not functioning efficiently, we become depleted, take on excess baggage, or both.

I am not using an analogy. This is literal fact. To understand it better, you need to understand nourishment.

Nourishment is a quantity of energy and wisdom combined that promotes Self-realization. We take in nourishment, and our body, energy and awareness come into a greater degree of harmony with Reality. Poor digestive capacity means we cannot recognize the nourishing quantity in food, be it physical food, emotional food, energetic food or wisdom food.

For instance, people with certain eating disorders often see food as toxic, or threatening. Likewise, people with a certain kind of limited karmic vision are offered nourishment in relationships but they can't recognize it. They often experience love and friendship as hurtful.

Self-realization is a process of remembering and recognizing your true nature. Taking in nourishment is intimately related to the process of Self-realization. You can't Self-realize if you aren't capable of taking in proper nourishment of every variety from gross to subtle.

A key point here is that we cannot digest what we cannot recognize. This is why although grace is raining down on us at every moment, most of us don't get it. This is also why we may receive good teachings and not be able to absorb them and put them to use.

Most of us have had the experience that we encounter a teaching when we are in a more limited condition, and we can only absorb a limited amount of the teaching. We do some more spiritual practice and come back to the teaching later. Now we "get" much more of it.

Our subtle digestive channels have opened, and we can now recognize and digest more wisdom.

On a gross level, this is why some of us have impaired digestive systems. Our physical-chemical system does not recognize what we put into our mouths as food. Western medicine has many names for these kinds of disorders, but from a Tantrik perspective, we are lacking the capacity to recognize what is nourishing.

When I was a young, Tantrik pup, I had a serious auto-immune digestive ailment. Food went in, but nourishment was not efficiently extracted from the food.

Shortly after I received initiation, I began a month-long sadhana suggested by my teacher to improve my health. I set up a little picture of the head of our lineage on my altar, and as I did the practice, I prayed to him for assistance. I told him that I wanted to Self-realize, and that I couldn't do the necessary work unless I was in better health. I asked him to grant me this boon.

After a month, the disease vanished and has never returned.

This is grace in action. Grace is a name for the most subtle form of nourishment. The boon of receiving and recognizing a more subtle form of nourishment corrected the gross physical aspect—my guts—as well. Usually we have to begin on the gross level and work toward the more subtle. Grace comes from the opposite direction. It is the subtle acting through the continuum on the gross expression or manifestation.

Digestion is one way to understand the difference between intellectual encounters with teachings and actually embodying the teachings. When we practice and digest teachings, we naturally display the wisdom virtues. The teachings are naturally revealed to be an aspect of our essence nature.

When we have only an intellectual understanding of the teachings, or when we are using the teachings to support fixation, we may sound like we know a lot, but our form of embodiment and our conduct do not reflect the teachings.

I want to end by talking for a moment about vegetarianism. Recently, a number of people have told me that they had to begin eating meat again after some period of time as vegetarians.

Meat is a grosser manifestation than are vegetables and other components of a vegetarian diet. Most of us, even if we are eating a balanced vegetarian diet, become depleted and deficient because our digestion cannot recognize and extract nourishment efficiently enough from a more subtle diet. We need meat because, excuse the silly word play, meat meets us where we actually live. And working at the level of our real situation is the hallmark of any authentic spiritual practice.

We've all heard stories about some highly Realized persons not needing to eat as much as a "normal" person. My *Satguru* (root teacher) Anandamayi MA went through long periods of her life eating very little. During these periods, she was healthy, energetic and even chubby.

Ma ate little, but was fully nourished because she was able to recognize, extract and digest the essence of nourishment from small amounts of food.

In fact, at one point Ma said that she had been experimenting with how efficiently she could extract nourishment from her surroundings and had discovered that she really didn't need to eat what we commonly call food. However, she also didn't want to upset those around her, so she continued to eat (Mukerji, *A Bird on the Wing* 77).

Tantra assists students to take in nourishment and digest more efficiently on every level. Eating a proper diet for your constitution and circumstance is just as important as learning how to take in nourishment through doing yoga or meditation.

Some people feel that starving oneself physically or otherwise is a component of a spiritual path. Nothing could be further from the truth. God is nourishment. If you starve yourself, you turn away from God—you turn away from your Self.

Siddhartha Guatama discovered this as a young man when he was engaging in a very austere practice. As he sat starving, freezing and burning, he finally realized the simple truth that we need to accept nourishment in order to fully discover Reality.

That is the moment when he fully entered into the path of becoming a Buddha.

SMALL I VS. EGO SMACKDOWN

Nothing is more of a spiritual cliché than the notion that you have to get rid of your ego. And nothing could be simultaneously more true and more false.

Ego means "I sense," but it is a limited, or small I, whose principle job is to defend your ignorance.

Anavamala is the root ignorance: your feeling of separation from others. Most of us embody the erroneous conviction that we are distinct individuals. Holding this conviction in our body, energy and mind, we spend our lives defending our individuality.

Our limited sense of I compels us to insist on "how I am," to protect and defend everything that I believe is "me" and "mine." This is ego's job.

Right now, stop reading and take a moment to feel your base anxiety. Many people are experiencing a quiet, or not so quiet hum of fear or anxiety all of the time. You can feel it in your whole body.

This is the fear that ego has of being attacked, malnourished, humiliated, abandoned and betrayed. It is the fear you have of losing this form when you die. It is the fear-hum of the vulnerability of your self-concept.

Individuality is a real experience, but we are not separate individuals. The ocean provides us with a living symbol of our condition. You can point to a wave and recognize it, but you cannot really say where a wave begins and ends. Waves are an individualized styling of ocean.

Just so, each of us is an individualized styling of Shiva nature. We are made of consciousness and energy, and we are an expression of consciousness and energy. Our forms are just as waves to the ocean of consciousness. We arise as these experiences, and then we subside. While we are manifest, we are always continuous with the whole.

There is no "skin" between us and the Lord, our own infinite Self.

Many times, you will hear teachers say that you have to kill your ego, or let the teacher do it for you. In one sense, this is true. We must surrender all defensiveness and the aggression we generate to defend our supposed boundaries.

However, simple I sense can never be surrendered, and you shouldn't try. Self-awareness is the nature of Reality. Shiva nature is pronouncing I AM in every leaf, beam of sunlight, toaster oven and variety of being.

Our I sense does not, and cannot be eradicated. But it can be liberated, released from its prison of separation. Tantrik *sadhana* (spiritual practice) helps you to relax the tensions of small I and opens you to realizing your identity with the I AM of Reality itself.

In this book, I do not use the word "ego." Instead, I refer to "small I" in order to remind you that your limited I sense is an aspect of the I AM of Shiva nature. There is no break between small I and its own essence and origin in the Lord. Small I is the cosmic I AM under a spell of forgetfulness. Tantrik sadhana breaks the spell.

So, yes, we do need to surrender our defensiveness, but in doing so, small I discovers it has been I AM all along.

WHAT IS SELF-REALIZATION?

The term Self-realization is pretty literal. It means recognizing and embodying your Self in the largest sense. Every day we realize small I. We embody small I all the time with our basic defensiveness and aggression toward life. Small I stays small by hanging onto fears, habits of separation and conceptual knowing. When we break out of the prison of small I, we begin to embody universal wisdom virtues such as compassion, devotion and clarity. We discover our fundamental continuity with life.

The pervasive, larger Self, of which our small self is an echo, has many names: Shiva nature, Buddha nature, Krishna or Christ consciousness or simply *that*. There is no need to get hung up on names, although we are naturally attracted to them. The many names for our essential nature make it possible for all of the varieties of beings in their unique conditions to be attracted to some version of the path of Self discovery. All of the names ultimately refer to the same Reality: pervasive, unbroken, wide awake livingness.

In any moment you have the potential to discover and embody more of the continuity of consciousness, more of the unbroken, wide-awakeness of the creation.

Even the smallest degree of Self-realization begins to show up right away in how you feel, relate and move through your everyday life. That is incontrovertible. And wondrous. To become Self-realized is a tall order, but it accomplishes itself incrementally. Luckily for us, or this would be a very dry and frustrating path!

Manifest life is a total, playful, startling, inventive, no-holds-barred conversation. Everything we encounter—all of our situations and so-called problems—are aspects of Reality's total responsivity and devotion to its own creations. But many human lives are structured around one kind of conversation: commercial exchange. I pay you for information, and then I go out and resell that. We buy and sell the right to pollute the planet. We strike deals in our relationships. I'm supposed to meet your needs in exchange for you meeting my needs.

Many of us are in a constant state of calculating potential gains and losses—whether these be emotional, intellectual, spiritual or material. Our experience is actually quite impoverished when we are only participating at this one, rather flat level. Nature's conversation is multi-dimensional and infinite. When we do Tantrik practice and reconnect with this rich conversation, we regain our capacity for experiencing natural wonder.

Tantrik sadhana engages us with time, space, mind, sound, vision, taste, touch and movement. These are the gateways through which the world conversation is happening. We can begin to recalibrate our bodies, energy and minds by introducing healthy rituals of eating, sleeping, working and relating into our everyday lives. When we do this, our subtle channels regain the capacity to bring us more precise insight into how Nature works. Our sense of wonder, devotion and tenderness blossoms. We can begin to participate in life with more skill and grace.

DON'T BELIEVE ME, OR ANYONE

The living, self-aware world provides human beings with uncountable methods for waking up to the cosmic fullness of our real nature. From the simplest devotional act, such as pouring water on the earth, to complex rituals; from solitary prayer to mantra and meditation, the spiritual practices we encounter in our human realm are natural technologies accomplishing the life process of the Lord. This uneven process leads us inexorably from states of relative ignorance to greater Self-understanding.

Many spiritual traditions are founded on faith, trust, belief and hope. These are valuable *bhavas*, or feeling orientations, for people who are attracted to those traditions. In the direct realization traditions of Kashmir Shaivism, Dzogchen, Chan Buddhism, and Daoism, however, faith, trust, belief and hope are definite impediments. Students in these traditions are advised to find out for themselves about the nature of Reality and to develop confidence in themselves and the life process. As my Guru Anandamayi Ma often said after she gave a teaching: *Now you go find out!*

And we *can* actually find out. We can find out what we are and how Reality works. We can become vastly more skillful in our interactions with the world. We can do this by relaxing our senses, including our minds, until the means and ways of our lives and our world become directly perceivable, until knowledge itself is revealed to be knowledge of Self, our own Self.

In order to actually find out, we must become explorers of our own nature, the nature of Reality. We must let go of the limited concepts about ourselves and the world that we have come to embody over the years and lifetimes. These repeating habits of limited understanding are our *karma*.

It's not easy to loosen our attachment to the ways we have always acted, felt and thought. It takes a certain quantity of energy and courage to open ourselves to experiencing Reality in a radically new, yet profoundly intimate way. All of us need help.

In the direct realization traditions, help comes in the form of a deep relationship with a teacher who has walked the path before us. The teacher's job is to deliver us to a direct, immediate encounter with our real nature. The job of the student is to bravely recognize what is being transmitted through the teacher and to do the work needed to erode the experience of limitation.

In the U.S., and elsewhere, contemporary people often feel that having a close relationship with a spiritual teacher is unnecessary. People hop around from one teacher to another, mixing and matching views and practices from different traditions. This is usually a strategy for preserving small self and its false sense of independence.

Other people worry about bad teachers or false Gurus. But why would anyone waste time fretting about bad teachers if there were not an underlying longing for a teacher to show you the way? In Reality, the practice of discipleship is a completely natural phenomenon. The co-arising relationship of teacher and student is the natural technology that Self has manifested in order to enact the play of waking up. Working together, step-by-step, teacher and student find the way home.

EMPTINESS AND FULLNESS

An experience of emptiness, or *shunya*, is assumed in some traditions to be the hallmark of Self-realization. Many students, and even teachers, misinterpret shunya to mean a state in which the mind is without thoughts, or a "realization" that the manifest world is literally an illusion, made of "nothing." Neither of these views is correct.

Shunya is the *experience* of emptiness we encounter when limited self and world concepts dissolve. For instance, if your house burns down, or your lover leaves you or, if in one moment, some cherished idea you have about yourself is overturned by your spiritual teacher, in that very instant of loss, you can discover shunya.

Shunya is the experience of the gap arising in the moment between a limiting concept being lost or ripped away and our efforts to regroup.

We go around acting as if our house is solid, safe and at least a semi-permanent refuge for our life. Then, in one hour, the house is burglarized, an earthquake demolishes it or it burns down. Our concepts about our house crash along with it.

Recall a moment such as this: the exact moment when you learned similarly shattering news. You may recall a feeling of profound destabilization, of something like free fall. This is the gap. The gap opens us to more Reality, to space, to vitality in the form of fear and openness. In this gap, we encounter a direct, embodied, nonconceptual experience of the impermanence of our concepts and the objects and relationships we charge with the burden of carrying those concepts for us.

If we are not practitioners, we do our best to scramble out of the gap as quickly as possible. We try to replace what has been lost—most importantly, we try to replace the things and people that gave us the feeling of permanence and safety. We try to "recover" from the trauma of shunya. As practitioners, we want to taste the gap as deeply as possible. We want to let go completely in the gap.

Many of the practices we do are designed to lead us to let go of limiting concepts of self and world and to experience their insubstantiality. When we have a wrong idea that shunya, or this experience of insubstantiality, is the fundamental nature of Reality, we try to hold onto the experience. Then shunya itself becomes a limitation on our Self-realization.

It is our limited understanding of Reality, that when destroyed, even if only for an instant, gives rise to the experience of emptiness.

If we let go and let the experience of shunya arise and subside naturally, we come into a completely different experience: Reality is not empty; it is full of consciousness and energy. We come into a direct and complete encounter with living presence.

This living presence is *made of* clarity, intelligence, wisdom, compassion, devotion and curiosity. It is pervasive omnipresence. It is God, and it is our own Self.

So let go, and find out.

Emptiness is an experience. Fullness is the state of the creation.

PRESENT AND PRESENCE

You often hear about the importance of "being in the moment" or "being present." Most of us interpret this to mean engaging fully with the present moment as opposed to being distracted by thoughts of the future or the past. We are being aware of what is happening right now rather than numbing out with fantasy.

In the direct realization traditions, the present as described above is the "ordinary present." It is an aspect of our experience of linear time. It is, of course, desirable to be engaged with the present moment rather than lost in thought or fantasy. There are some lovely practices designed to help students be more present in the ordinary sense. However, ultimately we are more concerned with *presence* than the present.

Being in presence means that all of our senses are open and awake. We are not grasping at successive moments in linear time with our mind. We are in a condition called *samavesha*, or immersion. We are fully immersed in the vital texture of livingness called Shiva nature: our own Self.

All direct realization practice aims at getting rid of the internalized watcher and becoming immersed in the direct experience of the play of consciousness and energy.

One of the first practices I teach my students is to feel the texture of the day. Before you get out of bed, you reach out with your mind and all of your senses. You have to use your mind as a sense organ, not in an analytic way. You use all of your senses, including mind and you try to capture a direct sense of the quality, the texture of the day ahead.

Is it heavy or light? Open or obstructed? Clear or cloudy? These are just a few examples. Beyond these simple qualities, it is possible to have very precise and direct perceptions about how consciousness and energy is expressing itself here and now. You can feel many things directly and receive communications. Then you can respond by adjusting your activities appropriately. This simple practice is a way you can begin to immerse yourself in the living presence of the Supreme Self.

MOTIVATION

The desire to practice emerges spontaneously from an infinite mandala of circumstances all moving you toward the revelation of a deep longing to know who or what you truly are.

TANTRIK TAPESTRY

IMAGINE YOURSELF STANDING in front of a beautiful Hindu or Buddhist painting depicting figures such as Gurus and deities. Perhaps hundreds of arms swirl around the deities, each hand curved into a different graceful mudra or brandishing a uniquely fearsome weapon for demolishing limitations. The Gurus assume yogic postures, or simply overflow with cosmic compassion. Detailed foliage grows along the borders. The painting is an orchestrated riot of rich mineral colors and luminous gold.

Now focus in on a smaller area of the painting. Move closer. There, another layer of world unfolds: smaller figures dance within the landscape of color, tiny Sanskrit mantras weave here and there. A ritual fire, a moon, a river, a yogi, a mountain abode are all rendered in meticulous detail.

Move even closer. Experience the bursting forth of yet another layer of life, another precise world realized in subminiature scale. Discover an entire planet of beings within the shaft of the Devi's hair, or the play of lotuses on the surface of a teardrop-sized lake.

Move closer yet again, and the consistent patterns that make up the complex whole come into view: the crosshatches, shadings, whispers of line and swirl, the infinite fields of grass-like brushstrokes hold multiple layers of creation bound tightly together on one piece of cloth.

Why all of these minute permutations? Why so many worlds within one world? The mandalas of life represented are revelations of Reality, born out of the direct insight of yogis and adepts. They are living symbols.

Normally we think of symbols as representing something. For instance, the word "apple" represents a fruit, but we could collectively choose a different word. In contrast, a living symbol is a real expression, or aspect of what it represents. The profuse and precise overflowing of Hindu and Buddhist works of art exemplify the many modes of appearing of the world essence. We can experience these works of art and directly learn something about how the world really is.

Try it. Look out across a landscape in nature. Take in the scene as one whole, then continually adjust your focus until you are "seeing" down into the intricate worlds that populate the whole. Doing this, you can have a direct experience that the mandala of the natural world and the mandala of the paintings are born of a single, continuous creative process. You can admire the unreserved, infinitely modulated creativity in both.

You may be aware of your reasons for feeling motivated to embark on a more conscious spiritual path. Many people begin because they want to alleviate some kind of mental, emotional or physical pain. Others begin because they experience the persistent feeling that life is missing some crucial ingredient not to be found in career, family or at the shopping mall. Relatively fewer people meet a teacher who inspires and moves them, or a tradition that captures their imagination or intellect.

Whatever your reasons are or were, eventually all motivation converges at the desire to know your Self. After all secondary motivations fall away, this single desire is revealed and begins to grow larger and larger in your life.

The desire to know who and what you really are is the same as the desire to know all of Reality because the Self, your Self, is pervasive and continuous. Your smaller experience of being a separate individual is actually a creative expression of the one Self. Hindu and Buddhist art reveals the infinite variety of this overflowing creativity and stimulates wonder and curiosity—two wisdom virtues of the enlightened Self.

The desire to reveal your Self fully to yourself is a natural desire; it is the power or Shakti that drives all beings inexorably toward what we call enlightenment. The limitations to Self-understanding that you now experience are aspects of the play of the world Self hiding and then unveiling, like a cosmic game of peek-a-boo.

As you walk the path of waking up to your own nature, you experience many small enlightenments along the way. Inevitably, you begin to notice more sharply the limitations to your understanding. This is at least somewhat painful, but absolutely necessary. Feeling the pain of being limited is an aspect of Self-realization.

Eventually, Self-understanding grows and you discover a strong desire to release these limitations. You understand better now how they restrict your spontaneity and participation with the world.

When some of these limitations begin to relax their grip on you, you express more natural curiosity about other people and the world. Curiosity is a wisdom virtue related to the Shakti, or energy of the cosmic drive for Self revelation.

At another stage, you are motivated by a strong desire to directly perceive and engage with more subtle manifestations of the creation. You may want to learn more about the laws of creation and how to work with them.

When the revelation of your own nature, the nature of the world Self, stands revealed even more, the devotional essence of Reality becomes paramount. A more profound and all-encompassing desire for surrender arises.

People always want to know why we must go through this process of experiencing relative ignorance before waking up. The answer is two-fold.

First, there is no answer because the question wrongly assumes that there is an explanation for everything in life. If we ask why a tree exists, well, of course we could go on about the forest ecology and the birds needing homes, or about the ways in which trees support the production of oxygen. But this would not explain why trees exist and not some other object that does the same job. Similarly, there is no external, overarching or final explanation for why Reality is exactly as it is.

On another level, the fundamental experience of Shiva nature is enjoyment of its own creations. We are having experiences of suffering and working hard to wake up. But from the perspective of Self-realization, even these experiences are enjoyable colors on the palette, or flavors in the banquet of life.

One way to begin to get a taste of this is to remember your enjoyment of sad, scary or even violent movies. Everyone in the movie is taking the drama very seriously, but you are enjoying. We think a movie is successful if it makes us cry or feel fear.

Reality is not a movie, but our movies are limited versions of the more expansive nature of Reality. When we begin to wake up, we start to feel the limitations of being stuck in our repetitive dramas.

We want to know who we really are and about the nature of the world. You could say that the difference between movies and Reality is that in Reality, Shiva is the actor, the director, the audience and the means of production. But of course movies are also Shiva nature, and when human beings make movies and enjoy them, we are "being Shiva" in our limited way.

AMBITION AND LONGING

Spiritual ambition is when we use our energy to strive for results in our sadhana that build up our self-image. For instance, we do our practice with certain goals in mind because we want to be known for having achieved those goals. But it is also true that *any* preconceptions about the outcome of sadhana are shaped by our limitations.

Spiritual longing, on the other hand, is the voice of God. Spiritual longing may cause us to work very hard in our practice, but we will be moving toward the limitless source of that longing, not toward some puny goal invented by small I.

Americans have the ambition *samskara* bad. (A samskara is literally a karmic "scar.") It's hard for us to really, really, really get it that life is not one long individualistic effort leading upwards and onwards to personal and professional glory. If we have one job, we've got our eye on another job. If we aren't looking too publicly successful, we suffer. If someone else knows more, makes more money, or attracts more attention, we experience jealousy and may even attempt to hurt the other person. Or we puff ourselves up extravagantly. We are almost always competing in some way, either subtle or gross.

Many people here treat their spiritual practice as yet another ladder of levels to conquer, or amazing experiences and powers to acquire. An astounding number of people begin their practice with the idea that they want to be teachers. Teachers relentlessly pursue money and fame.

Tantrik sadhana is a method for discovering an extraordinary life. This extraordinary is not something you can plan for, or create. You can't climb the ladder to extraordinariness. The extraordinary promised by Tantrik sadhana is not a career goal. In fact, the compulsive, competitive measuring of spiritual accomplishment causes any potential fruit to wither and rot on the vine.

The extraordinary is the spontaneous play of this life, experienced and embodied. In order to realize this, you must totally surrender any contrivance of self or world concept, including preconceptions about the fruits of sadhana. Remember: any goal you set for your practice before tasting the fruit of the practice will always fall short.

The process of letting go of your fundamental defensiveness requires that you follow primordial longing. When you meet an appropriate teacher, practice and tradition, your longing will in some way recognize the limitless home it was been searching for. By following the teacher and teachings without reservation, rather than willfully setting competitive goals in advance, you discover wonder, delight in life and contentment.

On the other hand, the ambition to get out of your practice what you have decided in advance you want, and the search for recognition and rewards from others, brings anxiety, disquiet, insecurity and disease. Because you remain dependent on maintaining self-image, you will not be willing to let go of what needs to be surrendered. Letting go will be even harder if your career is entangled with your spiritual practice.

In the *Bhagavad Gita*, Lord Krishna teaches that everything a yogi does is *yajña*—a devotional offering. This continual state of offering is exemplified by the mantra *svaha*. Svaha means: I surrender my small self, to the larger Self, the world Self. This is a description of the life quality of a real yogi, or yogini. Yajña is real yoga (Abhinavagupta, *Commentary*, chapters 4-5).

Being in a state of surrender does not mean powerlessness. When you surrender your small self, you let go of your identification with your limitations. You draw on the Shakti of the world. What it does mean is the dissolution of small-self interest and the spontaneous embodiment of devotion toward all of the creation. It means being in a state of unconditioned responsivity, immersed in the living presence we call Reality.

Spiritual ambition takes an enormous amount of energy to maintain. Enormous. Spiritually ambitious people may look like they are surrendering deeply, or doing a lot of *karma yoga* (selfless service). They put out big energy, big Shakti. But only a small percentage of that energy ends up nourishing them or the people around them. Most of the energy is syphoned off into maintaining self-image. A person may feel temporarily, even for years, pumped up by the amphetamine of achievements and public recognition. But eventually, exhaustion will take its toll.

Spiritual ambition creates energy starvation all around. It is the death knell of authentic spiritual practice. When you sincerely and bravely follow your longing, no matter where it leads you, contentment, or at least greater peacefulness begins to set in. The whole "problem" of what to do, how to do it, and what rewards "it" will bring, subsides.

A PERSONAL STORY

During my first visit to Varanasi, my Ganapatya Guruji there played a game with me in a beautiful way. His subtle *lila* (enlightened play) demonstrates how the cosmic process responds to a sincere student by creating opportunities for the student to recognize and play out her tensions and fixations.

Here is the story.

I arrived in Varanasi with plans to do a particular sadhana involving tens of thousands of mantras, days of seclusion, and a final all-day fire ceremony.

When I first told him of my plan, my Guruji immediately said: *This thing is not necessary.*

I replied that of course it was necessary. Such a sadhana is required.

He looked at me kindly. *Just do one day*, he said.

Oh no! I protested. *I must complete the whole thing!*

Ok, he agreed, *but only do 7,000 mantras a day.*

Once again, the "hero" said *No!*

At this point, my Guruji's energy shifted.

I will help you, he announced with great enthusiasm. *I will do the fire ceremony with you!*

But it takes all day, I pointed out. Guruji is not a young man.

I will do it! He jabbed his right index finger in the air, and this settled the point.

Guruji called one of his other students and began busily organizing everything as if my plan had all along been the best idea ever. Now, not only was I doing it, but the entire household was coming along for the ride!

I was to start the mantra practice the next morning. That night, I came down with a high fever of no discernible origin. I barely made it back to my room. Just before dawn, I dragged myself out of bed and began setting up for the first *puja* (ritual offerings).

Somehow, that day I made it through the intended number of mantras.

But the next morning, still feeling sick, I started again. Suddenly, there was a tremendous noise of banging and people yelling on the ground floor. Workmen began dragging something up the steps of my landlady's house. When they got to the floor above mine, the hammering and sawing commenced.

Tiredly, I interrupted my practice. The landlady was hovering just outside my door. She informed me that she was building an addition onto the top floor of her house.

But, I told you I came here to do practice. You said it was quiet!

It will only be four or five days of construction, she answered with a shrug.

I closed my door and sat down with a thump. I began doing the mantra once again. The noise continued, and it was soon joined by the clanging of industrial-sized pots and pans from the restaurant kitchen next door. I could feel my fever rising.

My fingers stopped turning the mala.

I completed exactly 7,000 mantras that day.

In the evening, I went to see my Guruji.

I felt some nervousness. Guruji had volunteered to conduct the fire ceremony with me. I considered this to be an enormous blessing.

Not only this, but the whole neighborhood now knew about it.

Would Guruji be angry that I had stopped the practice? What would everyone think?

As I neared Guruji's house, a young man I knew who worked at the shop next door yelled out: *What happened to your puja?*

I smiled wanly and kept going.

Inside, Guruji sat in his usual chair. Several people were gathered around him.

He smiled at me with no apparent surprise.

Guruji, may I speak with you?

He motioned the others to move aside and indicated that I was to sit next to him.

Tell me, he said.

I told him that I had stopped the practice, that I was ill, and that I intended to leave Varanasi and go somewhere less urban.

I told him how grateful I was that he had offered to do the yajna. And I apologized profusely for any trouble I may have caused him or the other students.

Guruji looked at me with melting tenderness, his head moving gently back and forth in the Indian way.

He said simply: *There are no conditions. No boundaries. You are free.*

And then he added, placing both of his palms on his heart and looking into my eyes: *I am so happy for you.*

I am so happy for you.

But this is not the end of the story.

The next day, I went to say goodbye before I caught the train to Rishikesh.

So, you are going to Rishikesh. What will you do there? Guruji asked me.

I will complete the mantra practice, I answered, not yet having learned my lesson, even after all that had happened.

Without missing a beat, Guruji declared: *I will help you. I will help you from here!*

In Rishikesh, I got even sicker. I spent most of the remainder of my trip in bed. I never completed the sadhana.

What kind of "help" is this? I grumbled. But I knew.

The sickness, which turned out to be dengue fever, lasted for many months, during which my long-time habit of engaging in "sick effort" largely burnt itself out. Now I approached my sadhana with greater playfulness and devotion, rather than as something to be accomplished for the greater glory of "me." The practice flowed easefully.

The beauty of this Guru-disciple process is that I was delayed from doing a fairly ambitious practice until I had relaxed more deeply and let go of some of my ambition.

When I saw Guruji again the next year, he looked at me and said: *You are much improved. I am so happy for you.*

FULLY HUMAN

Discovering the full potential of life in a human body is one of the core motivations for undertaking Tantrik sadhana. Right now, you are only able to experience a small percentage of your human potential. Some traditions glorify their teachers as divinities, or encourage students to have deities as teachers. In the Tantrik tradition, we say it is important to have a human teacher because we are learning how to be human.

Anandamayi Ma was constantly experimenting with the experience of being fully awake in a human body. She could do what we consider to be extraordinary things, such as be in two places at the same time, levitate or go without food and water. There was never any earnestness or pride connected to these experiments, only a bhava, or feeling of playfulness.

Ma was renowned for her capacity to heal people, to read the thoughts of others, see future events, perfectly perform rituals connected with spiritual traditions not her own, invoke mantras and scriptures in languages she had not studied and generally to interact with Reality on the most subtle levels. But most important of all was her great kindness, compassion and ability to host all experiences and people without exception and with unalloyed love. When I think of the human capacities I most want to embody as she did, it is these.

When we do not have much realization, we divide up the world into family, friends, acquaintances, lovers and strangers. The latter category includes nearly everyone. We easily become annoyed with or frightened by others. We find some people to be "crazy," or "weird," and we don't like those people. We are very, very lonely. Ma, and all realized people, show us that it is possible to live as a human being without being defensive or aggressive. We can relax our tensions and become fountains, showering everyone with compassion.

We don't have to travel to a heaven to do this. We can do it here.

All Tantrikas are also preparing for the dissolution of this human form and the completion of the human experience. What does it mean to complete the human experience? Well, it means relaxing so deeply that your karmic entanglements no longer bind you to this form. You are free to go, or to stay. Those who choose to stay are called "Jivanmukti" or "Mahasiddha." Such beings bring great benefit to everyone simply by remaining with us.

Most of us have extremely limited notions of Self-realization. These ideas usually involve visions of the individual small self accumulating powers and pleasures without giving up its sense of autonomy and self-importance. Most people find it difficult to envision realization outside of this box of small I.

Self-realization does, on one level, mean freedom. The freedom of Shiva nature is unlimited, unconditioned and playful creativity. Freedom of Self-expression is the nature of real freedom. We can only experience freedom of expression when we are in a state of profound nonattachment. If we are not, our expression will not be free or playful. It will be conditioned by likes and dislikes, by anxieties and specific cravings. It will be serious and self-important. Simply having powers does not make one free. While you are at the stage of sadhana, this freedom flickers, sometimes feebly, sometimes powerfully, between the cracks or gaps in your routine habits and compulsions. Sadhana helps you to relax in the gaps, where freedom is shining. Day-by-day, you begin to feel less afraid and constrained.

THE RETURN TO IMPERMANENCE

Hanging around spiritual types, you hear a lot about impermanence. I confess, I never "got" why anyone finds impermanence to be such an earth-shattering revelation.

Is being traumatized by impermanence a guy thing? Just a thought.

I was standing in line at a local organic grocery store. Apropos of nothing, the woman behind me proclaimed: *I feel sorry for bugs. Their lives are so short!*

Remember, this was Berkeley, California. Eighty-seven percent of the people are thinking stuff like this instead of looking in their rear view mirrors and using their turn signals.

I hate to break it to you, I answered helpfully, *but humans don't live much longer than bugs.*

Acknowledging one's own inevitable death does put things in perspective. We should all do this frequently. One of the best answers to the question "Why do sadhana?" is "I could die at any moment." Putting off sadhana today might mean putting it off for a long time. Banana slugs have a hard time remembering their mantras.

But our fear of impermanence is a lot more insidious than worrying about the big D.

Every idea we hang onto about ourselves, others, the world or anything, is like trying to immobilize a speck of dust in a wind tunnel. Everything we do to shore up our sense of small, individual self is a mark of our fear of impermanence. Life in samsara is change, and we resist life at every turn. Most of us are basically Blobs of Resistance.

One of the most stunning things about Tantra is that it already knows itself to be impermanent and provisional. Impermanent in that our Gods, rituals and organizations will die, and others will come along. Impermanent because in order to Self-realize, each practitioner must eventually surrender even the concepts and attachment to practices that make up the tradition. We need them now to support us in our practice, but they eventually fall away as we become more awake and immersed in our own unlimited livingness. This experience cannot be described by any categories, concepts or system. Practicing Tantra faithfully will lead you to this realization.

Have you ever heard of such a thing? A spiritual tradition that preaches, and teaches, its own provisionality? I find this unspeakably beautiful. The lack of dogmatism within Tantra reflects the nature of Nature revealed through Tantrik sadhana. This is Tantra at its finest.

The *Vijñana Bhairava Tantra* as revealed by Swami Lakshman Joo, a modern siddha and interpreter of Kashmir Shaivism, teaches that the descriptions of reality used in his own tradition are *meant for the spiritual advancement of the unenlightened. . . .*

> *You have to take a medicine which is not sweet. It is*
> *bitter. It is not tasty. You do not like to taste it. Then*
> *what does your mother do? She puts something sweet*
> *in your mouth first, and says, 'Take it now'. (12-13)*

The "bitter medicine" is that we really must lose all of our cherished ideas about ourselves and the world. The "sweets" are all of the necessary supports that we use along the way to help us to realize.

And they are sweet, are they not? I am speaking about our teachers, rituals and cosmological categories. I am talking about cherished yet limited ideas such as those of freedom and openness.

We detach from our limiting karmic habits and fixations and attach to our teachers, *ishta devatas* (tutelary deities), sadhana, traditions, organizations, philosophy, and whatever else moves us. In this way, we form new patterns or samskaras. The old patterns were moving us in the direction of deeper karmic entanglement. The new patterns move us in the direction of less entanglement. Tantrik sadhana works on the principle of *we rise by that which we fall*. In other words, we are good at forming habits, so we use that skill to form habits that free us rather than bind us.

For a long time, lifetimes perhaps, we are extremely motivated by these new samskaras. Their energy is brilliant and enlivening. We are deeply in love with our teachers and traditions. But in the end, even these samskaras must go. When that happens, we can be totally at home, fearless and loving in the world of impermanence. We can just enjoy impermanence without being conditioned by it because our base will be the unendingness of Shiva nature. We can relate playfully to impermanence as a wonderful display or ornament of our own nature. If we feel like doing ritual, we can do that. But now our activities are performed solely as expressions of the pure, unimpeded devotion of Shiva nature to itself.

So, rather than rejecting or feeling sad about impermanence and desperately seeking salvation, Tantra gives us the means to make the return home to impermanence. We recognize impermanence as the ongoing expression or life process of Shiva nature, and we enjoy that.

DOUBT

Many practitioners fear their own doubt, or they think something is wrong if they doubt themselves, their teachers or the teachings. The open secret is that 99.99 percent of spiritual aspirants experience doubt.

As the highly-accomplished practitioner Abhinavagupta taught, doubt is actually a condition of relative openness. If we are either very ignorant, or very sure of ourselves, we are not open to learning. Doubt is a soft feeling, although it can be uncomfortable (*Commentary 5*).

Crazy wisdom teachers purposefully create doubt in their disciples. Doubt happens when a student holds some defensive, or habitual fixed concepts about himself, about teachers, or Reality. When these are skillfully challenged, doubt arises and opens a gap in a limited worldview. The student feels fear and a kind of emptiness. If surrender happens, the gap can become real spaciousness. Now the student can experience being in the immediacy of life and just exploring and discovering rather than projecting.

Some people experience a kind of habitual worrying about themselves. This is not the kind of doubt I am talking about. This kind of worry is an activity, like playing computer games or constant mental planning, whose purpose is to distract you from experiencing the groundlessness of life.

If you use worry in this defensive way, you need to learn that *don't know* is an authentic, honorable and relaxing place to sit. Just sit and cultivate having contact with the underlying experience that you don't know about yourself, others or life. Fear will arise and then eventually subside. Don't run away from the fear or try to fix it. Just let it be.

Over time, you will begin to feel that not knowing about yourself is fine. You will experience deep relaxation at this point. Accustom yourself to just sitting in the relaxation of *don't know*. Now you are directly encountering your real circumstance, and you can do sadhana and begin to discover.

USE EVERYTHING

God is the totality of the life process. Because all of life is an expression of Shiva nature, Tantrikas can use every aspect of life, everything that is presented to us, just as it is, in order to help us discover our real nature. We can bring every aspect of life onto the path because all phenomena, even suffering, contain the wisdom seeds of enlightenment.

We can perform complicated *kriyas* (generally internal yoga using breath, chakras and channels), or meditate on the moment after a sneeze. We can work with the energy of joy, as well as the energy of jealousy, anger, hatred, fear and disgust. We can practice while on retreat in a cave, as well as while walking in a city park. We can use our relationships, our eating, our movement, our work and play as fields of practice and gateways to realization. Everything becomes sadhana. Nothing and no one is left out. This is called *"abhyasa"*: unbroken practice.

Abhyasa is not just about spiritual talk, or sentiment. It's not about concepts. As the saying goes, *Words don't cook rice.* Doing unbroken practice means remembering to use the tools of your tradition at all times, especially when you find yourself sliding comfortably into fixation and reactivity.

It takes awareness, courage, commitment and effort to pull yourself away from limited habits of body, emotion and mind. And to do it over and over again, not just when you are sitting on a meditation cushion, but *everywhere.* This kind of process of waking up takes great effort.

We must undertake this effort without a complete understanding of the fruits of our effort. No matter what anyone tells us, what we think we are working toward, what we want, or what we read about the process in books, the fruit only becomes visible as we experience it, day-by-day, step-by-step.

Shiva nature expresses itself along a continuum of more subtle to more coarse experiences. When I use words such as "coarse" or "gross," I mean both something more tangible and the aspects of everyday experience that are most ordinary and accessible. Using whatever is ready-to-hand, we walk backwards, we return. What do we return to? We return to take refuge in our own unconditioned, unlimited nature. This is what "sits behind" all manifestations and gives rise to them out of its own subtle body of consciousness and energy.

STOP SEEKING NOW

My brother used to call me the "searcher seeker." This label could be applied to most people on a spiritual path. We spend a lot of time desperately seeking something even if we aren't quite sure what that something is.

Judging from the world's many spiritual autobiographies, the searcher seeker isn't a uniquely Western phenomenon. It's an expression of how human beings start to wake up. But what happens when the searcher seeker comes from a particularly aggressive, materialistic culture in which never-ending growth is the predominant value?

The seeking never stops.

Seeking "bigger, better, and more" is a national, cultural disease in the U.S. We're always trading up, moving forward, climbing the ladder, expanding and acquiring. No one is happy without a plan to get More, or be More. We demand that our kids to carry on the More tradition. We've even got a new profession, the life coach, to help people succeed on the More path.

What is the result of this endless, compulsive seeking and searching? Anxiety. Misery. Depression. Aggression. Anger. Jealousy.

Why? Because we are so compelled to seek more, we have lost the ability to recognize enough. We have lost touch with the feeling of fulfillment.

Applied to spiritual practitioners, this means that many people find it difficult to recognize when they have met an appropriate teacher, to stick with that teacher, and to relax and take refuge in the teachings. We may fleetingly feel the compassion of the teacher and the wisdom of the teachings. We may even talk as if our teacher and the teachings are the best, the highest, and so on, thereby pumping ourselves up to think we have finally arrived. But we cannot stop the momentum of seeking, and so we cannot fully relax and be truly nourished by our present situation.

We are like people at a party. Our gaze obsessively darts around the room and never focuses on the conversation at hand. We are constantly looking past the teacher, the teachings and our current practice. We move around between one teacher and another, and one tradition and another. We go to one teacher and ask what they think about the teachings of another teacher so we can sit back and judge, masking with cleverness our own lonely feelings of separation. We collect initiations and empowerments. We console ourselves with the lists of teachings we have attended by famous teachers and brag, using the names of our "famous" teachers as spiritual status trading cards.

We never complete one practice before we are on to the next one, or we mix and match practices from different teachers because we have to have it all, like a bagel with everything.

When I first came into a conscious relationship with my Guru, I knew beyond any ordinary analysis or thinking that there was no more need to seek. Yet, for a time, the habit of seeking continued. I fretted about whether or not to go to this or that teacher, collecting more practices along the way.

I had what I had always longed for. Only a kind of anxious momentum—that cultural karma of following the path of More—kept me from entirely surrendering. Luckily, the profound relaxation that derives from recognizing Guru and taking refuge in her finally taught me what lifetimes of compulsive seeking could not.

Gaining back the memory and taste of fulfillment is a crucial moment in any person's unfoldment. Deep surrender, and the supreme offering of Self to Self, emerges only from this.

Of course, not every person who goes from teacher to teacher, or from tradition to tradition, is doing so compulsively, or out of fear. But these "honey bee yogins" are a more rare phenomenon than you might think. Most of us do not have the capacity to draw nourishment in this way. Having multiple teachers and even traditions is a distraction. We create a paradoxical situation of excess that is driving us to starvation.

One of the unique features of direct realization Tantrik practice is its focus on tasting moments of fulfillment in everyday life. For instance, after eating a meal, we take some time to relax, recognize and enjoy the feeling of contentment and fullness. We can do this after hearing beautiful music, or immediately after any fulfilling experience. When we stop to savor these moments, we are recognizing and consciously embodying something fundamental about the essence state of Shiva nature. There are potentially many moments such as these in a day, many such opportunities to realize more of your enlightened nature embedded in the fabric of ordinary life.

GURUS AND DISCIPLES

Gurus and disciples arise together as one ornament of Shiva Nature. Together they are a natural technology for playing the game of revealing the nature of the Self to the Self.

GURU YOGA

THE RELATIONSHIP TO Guru is the central practice of direct realization Tantra. In the mirror of your relationship with Guru, you see yourself as you are showing up in the moment with all of your karmic tensions, and at the same time, you see your enlightened, eternal essence.

The Tantrik tradition has a huge number of practices, from ritual to mantra, hatha yoga, kriya yoga, yantra and mandala. But in the end, it all comes down to what is called "Guru yoga." "Yoga" means union, and Guru yoga means the practice of union with the Guru. Through this alchemy of Self, you can have the recognition that the enlightened essence of Guru is the same as your own.

In the *Kularnava Tantra*, Lord Shiva says: *He who makes one know: 'I am the knower of the essence of all the Vedas, I am the heart', who is inseparable from God and who is ever-pleased in heart'* – he is the *Guru* (Rai 251).

The Guru is not apart from you, existing to be worshipped. She helps you to know the continuity of consciousness. Through transmission, or the natural alchemy of the Guru-disciple experience, you discover that the essence of the teachings, and the heart of Reality, is your very own Self.

The simplest form of Guru yoga is to constantly remember your teacher. If your teacher is capable of reflecting essence nature, when you are around her, you will feel something special in yourself. By remembering her, you can bring on that special feeling of relaxation and spaciousness wherever you happen to be and in any situation.

Try to be in a state of constant remembrance of your Guru. If you have a mantra given to you by that teacher, try to do it while out and about, and especially when you are in a stressful situation with another person.

Keep your Guru's face and words and teachings with you at all times, as much as possible. Saturate yourself in their way of being, their state of realization. Feel that you are taking refuge in your true home. Ask for help when, inevitably, your karmic fixations win the day.

If you do this, little by little, over time, the qualities of that person will arise in you.

There are more complicated or formal types of Guru yoga, but they all have the same fruit: to recognize and begin to embody more of Shiva nature through the gateway of your relationship with Guru.

Upon learning that Guru yoga is the central practice of Tantra, the eyes of some people glaze over. Ears shut down. Skepticism sets in, even resentment.

Most of the Western-style re-inventions of Asian spiritual traditions involve either the importation of psychological models of the self, or the substitution of community or "inner" Guru for a real-life teacher. Inner Guru is not just common sense, or what feels good to you. True Guru, of any kind, will kick your butt and challenge your common sense ideas about everything.

In my experience, most of the people who reject living teachers and claim that they are following what they call "inner Guru," or who say: *the whole world is my Guru*, are beginners on the path. They are just not ready to give up what they erroneously feel is their independence.

As Dzongsar Kyhentse Rinpoche says, *Guru is the person you hire to dismantle you.* How many of us have the wisdom, skill, clarity, and courage to do this without the help of a living teacher who has walked the path before us? And why would we want to try? That is the crucial question (Patten, DVD).

When you are directly accessing Guru without the aid of a human teacher, you will understand the grace and beauty of the phenomenon of Guru. You won't complain about or denigrate human teachers. In fact, the opposite will be true: you will be suffused with wonder and gratitude that teachers exist at all. And you will compassionately desire all beings to feel the grace of Guru raining down on them.

A human Guru is a manifestation of *Guru Tattva*. "Tattva" means "element" or "function." Guru Tattva is the pervasive element of cosmic wisdom energy, that moves us toward Self-realization. While it is absolutely true that Guru can be recognized in anything, the human Guru is a naturally arising phenomenon that most people find easier and more effective to relate to during the many stages of their unfolding.

The primary function of Guru is to serve as a mirror in which we can recognize ourselves. The mirror can manifest in many different ways because a Guru will do anything to help us Self-realize. Oftentimes "anything" is painful. However, a true Guru is not being mean or authoritarian to satisfy her own needs. What really moves us about a true Guru is her great compassion.

Looking into the face of the open, infinite compassion of Guru, all of our limitations, and our infinite potential, become clear. In the presence of Guru, we can sense the distance between our state of tension and the open state of Realization. This distance seems very far and, at the same time, no distance at all because Guru is showing us our very own enlightened nature.

In the presence of Guru, everything for which we have ever longed reveals itself. At the same time, Guru is not a savior. In the presence of Guru, we discover total responsibility for our condition. We look at the Guru, and we know, "this is what I truly am." We know that only we ourselves can take the steps needed to relax our tensions and open to life. Guru shows us this in the mirror of Guru.

It is possible to be in the presence of a great Guru and not recognize Guru. A human Guru cannot force anyone to look into the mirror. She can only be that for those who are ready. A person's recognition of Guru is an exquisitely-timed cosmic event.

Many people have teachers, but they have not met Guru. Their relationship with their teacher is quite ordinary. A person goes along, learning many useful things and growing, but their world has not yet been fundamentally and irrevocably altered.

Meeting and recognizing Guru is a cataclysmic event in the life of a person, even if it is a quiet cataclysm. At this moment, you will become conscious of the fact that all of your pretenses—your decisions, analyses, doubts, worrying and problematizing—are just so much dust in the wind. You will still keep trying to build a life out of that dust, but somewhere inside, you will already know it is futile.

You will recognize that the expanded state of the Guru is your real destination. And despite the waxing and waning of your re-sistances and doubts, you will know with certainty that you will indeed come home.

The recognition of the inevitability of Self-realization is one of the most shattering, and relieving, aspects of what one learns by looking in the mirror of Guru. We feel shattered because we know that our attachments will fall by the wayside, and we are not quite ready to let go. We are profoundly relieved because we finally know what we are and that we cannot be left behind.

TRANSMISSION

Transmission is the key to the Guru yoga of direct realization traditions such as Kashmir Shaivism, Dzogchen and Chan Buddhism. Transmission is an experience of deeper realization revealed to the student, generally through the medium of a teacher.

Transmission happens through touch, voice, glance and visions, mind-to-mind and in dreams. Transmission helps students who are still largely bound to dualistic experience find their way back to an experience of greater continuity with life. Whether we talk about the *darshan* (gaze) of the Guru, "getting" *shaktipat* (hands-on transmission), receiving an empowerment or seeing our original face, all transmission is a gateway to greater participation in Reality.

One common misunderstanding is that during transmission, the teacher gives the student energy that the student lacks. This is wrong View. All energy is *the* energy of the body of God. It doesn't belong to the teacher any more or less than it belongs to you. However, teachers with some realization do have access to more energy because they are participating in a larger, less individualized body. If the teacher is still operating with various tensions of small I, then she might want to (falsely) claim this energy for her "self."

What happens in a transmission situation is that the teacher presents you with the possibility of experiencing enlightened qualities of the natural state within, or for yourself. It is something like removing an obstacle, or opening you to a shared experience. The relatively more realized state of the teacher acts as a catalyst for you to taste that directly in you.

A teacher may give formal transmission, but transmission is continuously happening when a teacher is highly realized. If you know how to relax and be in a state of Guru yoga, just being around your teacher in any ordinary moment is of great benefit.

In truth, the entire world is continuously "transmitting" the natural state. Most people aren't conscious of this due to heavy conditioning, but revealing Self-knowledge through transmission is a world capacity that uses particular people and situations as conduits for our benefit.

Why is transmission so important? Because students must recognize and begin to more fully embody the natural state in order to progress in sadhana. Through transmission, teachers give students "tastes" of the fruit of sadhana so that students can remember and work toward that. With transmission, you can begin practice with some embodied understanding, not just conceptual knowledge. You know where you are headed.

LET'S PLAY GURU AND DISCIPLE!

The student and teacher together are a cosmic process: a function or a capacity. One is not separate from the other. Student and teacher are one situation. The student and teacher together are an expression of the game or play of world Self-recognition.

Instead of thinking of a student and a teacher primarily as people, think of studenting and teachering. Studenting and teachering are dependent; one cannot exist without the other.

What we call a "student" is a person through whom the cosmic capacity for studenting is expressed. What we call a "teacher" is a person through whom teachering flows. In your role as a student, you should often ask yourself: "Am I making myself available to studenting?" You should work to open to the world flow of studenting.

A great Guru is greatly available to the world process of Guru. A great Guru is like a clear and clean river through which teachering becomes available to anyone who steps into that never-ending, compassionate flow.

A great Guru and a great disciple together, as one process, demonstrate all of the cosmic virtues. All compassion, all selflessness, all equanimity, all yoga.

A great Guru and a great disciple are really one and the same. Virtues of service, dedication, compassion and surrender to the world process flow from this complete situation. Everyone benefits from coming into contact with a great teacher and her disciple.

When you participate wholeheartedly in the cosmic studenting-teachering process, devotion to one teacher ends in your embodiment of natural devotion to all of the creation. The teacher is your gateway to discovering this.

Sri Anandamayi said to her disciples: *You all have wanted it [me] and you have it now. So play with this doll for a little while* (qtd. in Lannoy 8).

Mataji is declaring that her availability, her manifestation is the responsiveness of the world to itself. She is a "doll," a piece in the cosmic game. Now, let's play! Make use of this process!

GURU KULA

In ancient times and continuing today, most Tantrik Gurus have relatively few students with whom they are working intensively. Each teacher-student relationship is unique, and each student requires individualized sadhana and close supervision. In order for the natural technology of teacher-student to work its best magic, teachers and students must live in close proximity, usually for a number of years.

In fact, the best method for most dedicated students of householder teachers is that they live with, or very near to their teachers for some time. This is called the "Gurukula" system. Students become members of the teacher's family.

The practice of having daily contact with your teacher is *tapas*, or austerity. It supercharges your practice, confronts you directly with your fixations and helps you to relinquish tensions via the immersion plan.

Students who have more fully discovered the desire to Self-realize do everything possible to remain in the presence of their teachers. Others come and go, trying to "manage" the inexorable life process by regularly escaping to the comfort of more familiar habits, away from the fire of transmission.

Not many students are ready for a full-on teacher-student relationship, and teachers, who are also human, cannot generally provide this function to very many students.

Sometimes teachers have one or a few students and that is all. More common, especially these days, is that teachers have numbers of "come and go" students and only a few for whom they function as a Tantrik Guru, if they are qualified to do that.

Anandamayi Ma spent decades traveling up and down India, bringing moments of greater peace and contentment to people who would never be her close students. She answered questions and offered advice and comfort. But she initiated and directly guided the sadhana of relatively few people during her lifetime.

Despite competitive social scenes in yoga classes and mass initiations, the heart of the tradition is still one teacher working together with one student and finding a way home.

SPIRITUAL COMMITMENT

You can break a dinner engagement. You can leave a marriage. You can even dump your Guru, or relinquish a formal vow or initiation. But you cannot ever break the commitment to realize your own essential nature. This "natural commitment" is built into the life process itself. You can be ignorant of this, or you can consciously participate by doing sadhana, but either way, everything you do will express the desire to discover your real nature.

For instance, a person who self-medicates by drinking or taking drugs is trying to relieve the suffering caused by feelings of separateness. The *sadhika* is doing exactly the same by undertaking spiritual practice.

A person who lashes out in anger is drawing a line of connection between herself and another person. So too, a *Tantrika* (person who practices Tantra) is trying to realize the continuity of all life.

Everything we do has the same goal. The difference between one activity and another lies only in whether it emerges from greater or lesser limitation of View and whether it drags us into deeper ignorance, or moves us toward waking up.

In the end, though, even the most harmful activities offer opportunities to choose the path of greater relaxation and realization. This merciful natural law is the reason why people often express gratitude for illnesses, trauma and other difficult experiences. A person who is a little bit aware can understand and benefit from the growth inherent in such situations.

Any particular spiritual commitments we make along the way—such as commitments to do practices or commitments to teachers through the process of initiation—are actually re-affirmations of the natural commitment to awakening that is born in the blood. We may, and should if we are maturing spiritually, feel enormous love for and gratitude toward our teachers. But when we take an initiation, or make a commitment to a practice, we should do it with devotion to discovering *our own* essence. If we do so, we can complete every vow and fulfill the promise of every initiation. Then, when and if we move on, there will be no karmic baggage to carry with us.

ASK, AND YE SHALL ASK AGAIN

Spiritual traditions serve up many stories of disciples who go to extraordinary lengths to get teachings from Masters. Milarepa, a Tibetan Mahasiddha, wanted to receive teachings from a Guru named Marpa. Marpa made Milarepa build stone houses, tear them down and rebuild them many times over before agreeing to teach the faithful disciple.

The kriya yoga folks love to tell the story of a certain aspirant who climbed the Himalayan mountains seeking teachings from the immortal Babaji. When the determined devotee finally found the Mahasiddha and his band, Babaji ordered him to jump off the side of the mountain, a deadly deed that was accomplished without the slightest hesitation. Babaji then asked his disciples to collect the mangled remains of the aspirant. Declaring the young man to be worthy, Babaji brought him back to life and permitted him to stay and learn.

While most of us might choose to delay enlightenment a few thousands lifetimes rather than go to these lengths, less extreme tests of our commitment to Self-realization are a usual feature in the lives of students of Tantra.

In the Tantras, we are admonished to test a teacher thoroughly before taking initiation. However, once we choose a teacher, it is our turn to be tested before the deal is sealed. You will also be tested at many other stages of your journey with your teacher.

Every teacher has her or his own methods. At each stage, the teacher wants to know if you are capable of opening and committed to growing, or not. Two of the most common forms of testing are to refuse to give teachings, or to put obstacles in the way of receiving teachings.

Chogyam Trungpa Rinpoche, a Tantrik Buddhist master, once told a student not to let anyone into a certain teaching who was not already a member of the community. He simultaneously told another student to invite anyone and everyone!

When a lot of new people showed up, they were met at the door by a stern student telling them the teaching was closed. Eventually, only one new student persisted in staying at the teaching. Persistence and boldness, along with a respectful method of approach, are indications of the general capacity that students bring to a situation. Rinpoche was quite pleased with his new student. (Mt. Shasta, "A Trungpa Rinpoche Crazy Wisdom Teaching")

If you meet a teacher you respect and recognize as important to your self-realization, but you give up after asking for teachings only one time, the opportunity may pass you by. If you are timid, or not really motivated, you won't persist. Teachers are keenly aware of all of these indications and will respond accordingly.

A phenomenon I've noticed here in the U.S. concerns students who make a declaration that someone is their teacher, or who actually formally ask someone to be their teacher. These actions are then followed by a total, or near-total cessation of effort. Having showed up at the doorstep, they expect the teacher to invite them in, offer them a cocktail, serve them a seven-course meal and tuck them into bed afterward.

The real situation is quite the reverse. Once you recognize someone as your teacher, whether it be for that week or the next 17,000 lifetimes, that's when you should be ready to work, and work hard. If you ask for teachings and get them, be prepared to follow through with everything you've got.

You are responsible for your realization. A teacher cannot liberate you. Any teacher who personally promises to give you liberation should be abandoned, and quickly. A teacher can only give you tools for self-realization, the guidance of a good spiritual friend and the opportunity to taste, through the gateway of her own being, the natural state. The rest is up to you.

GURU IS DIFFERENT FROM TEACHER

Teachers abound, and how wonderful that is! Throughout the course of our lives, we encounter many people who serve as teachers for us. In fact, every person and every life situation can potentially be a teacher. However, teacher is not necessarily Guru.

Some people say: *I don't need a Guru. Life is my Guru.* This can be true, but experiencing all of life as Guru occurs in advanced stages of spiritual unfoldment. In many cases, a person saying this is simply not ready for the challenge to small I of relating to a real Guru.

When we learn a skill or a craft from someone, the Sanskrit term for that person is *upaya* teacher. The definition of upaya is "skillful means." For instance, most yoga teachers in the West are upaya teachers. They are able to impart some techniques, but they do not have much realization. Most of the teachers we encounter in schools and workplaces are upaya teachers.

You also hear people say: *My cat is my Guru, or my children are my Gurus.* In most cases, cats and children are not highly realized beings. But we can see things about ourselves and learn from looking in the mirror of our relations with anyone. This mirroring function is an important aspect of a real Guru-student relationship. The difference is that with a real Guru, the mirror is fully awake.

You can also encounter upaya Gurus. These are people with at least some degree of realization from whom you receive particular practices, but you are not relating to that person more broadly as your spiritual preceptor.

The word "Guru" means "dispeller of darkness." Limited View, or ignorance of one's real nature, is the only darkness. The Guru is someone who can aid you in dispelling limited View.

In the *Guru Stotram*, the disciple sings: *Salutations to that glorious Guru who, when I was blinded by ignorance, applied medicine and opened my eyes.*

The "medicine" is the transmission and the teachings. The Guru helps you to see in the largest sense. She shows you the way to open all of your senses, including your eyes and your mind, so that you can participate in your life with the most exquisite, expansive subtlety.

In the classical Tantrik tradition, when we speak of impurity, what we mean is the darkness of limited realization. There is no idea of sin or wrong-doing attached to limited View. In fact, even your experience of limitation is enlightened Shiva nature showing up as that experience. You are Lord Shiva tasting the experience of limitation.

The other common meaning of "Guru" is "heavy." The Guru is heavy because she keeps insisting on prodding, pushing and poking you to surrender your limitations. You want to surrender and you don't want to surrender, both at the same time. The Guru's "help" can feel very heavy at times. But you should always be aware of the Guru's compassion, no matter how heavy the going gets.

The 14th century wandering yogini, Lalla or Lalleshvari, wrote:

> When I was with my teacher, I heard a truth
> That hurt my heart like a blister,
> the tender pain of seeing something I loved as an
> illusion. (19)

Anandamayi Ma, upon being told that her eyes were causing total devastation to people who encountered her, responded: *Am I really causing total devastation? If you people really underwent a total devastation, that would be something extremely good* (*Ananda Varta* 34.1: 3)

Guru is a function, a technology, a gateway and a mirror. Guru is the Supreme Self manifesting as a person in a way that allows less realized people to experience that Supreme Self as themselves. If you are a little bit open, you will notice that being around a Guru feels different from being around other people. It may be somewhat shocking, or at least unnerving. You will definitely feel moved and answered in a way you have been longing to be answered.

I remember a teaching given by Khenpo Tsultrim Gyamtso Rinpoche that I attended early on in my life as a Tantrika. The state of Rinpoche was so expansive, all of my tensions were painfully highlighted against the backdrop of his greater realization. I was in a kind of "transmission shock," receiving both greater awareness of my fixations and, simultaneously, a river-like experience of the condition of the teacher as my own essence. I only spent a few hours with Rinpoche, but the experience opened the door for me to a new level of embodied understanding.

As Ma said, real darshan is: *to see That which when seen the wish to See anything more vanishes forever, to hear That which when heard the desire to hear anything else does not awaken anymore (Matri Vani II 105).*

NO SHAME NO BLAME

Tantra is often called "the fast path" to discovering your real nature. Much of this "fastness" happens between you and your teacher. The teacher does everything in her power to provoke, disturb and generally pull the ground out from underneath your feet.

The neat little package of stories, concepts and fixations you call "you" has to be opened up so you can see your real situation. You might feel things are getting uncomfortably messy. From the teacher's perspective, you are beginning to experience spaciousness.

Teachers in the direct realization traditions like to tell different versions of this story. A certain disciple had been studying with his teacher for many years. The day had come for him to go out on his own.

For the first time, the teacher invited his disciple to dinner. The student washed and dressed in his best clothes. He bought a gift and knocked at his teacher's door. The teacher opened the door.

Immediately, the student smelled alcohol on his teacher's breath! His teacher was dirty, disheveled and a cigarette dangled from his mouth. The teacher welcomed the student in. The house was a filthy wreck. Books, papers, clothing, and empty bottles of wine and other liquors covered every surface. In the doorway to the kitchen stood a woman. The teacher said: *Meet my girlfriend!* The student had always assumed his teacher was celibate, even though the teacher had never said this himself.

A lightning bolt of shock hit the disciple. He was overcome with feelings of anger and betrayal. Then the disciple looked up into his teacher's face. He saw there the same indescribable tenderness, compassion and wisdom that had been his mirror, guide, mother and father through all of the long years of sadhana. He realized that the freak-out was his teacher's parting, compassionate gift.

A spiritual freak-out is the last stand of a hardened fixation, or self-concept throwing a tantrum as it passes away. After the freak-out ends, you are left in a state of greater openness. Now the student could see this tension and relax more deeply. In the Tantrik way, being freaked out by your teacher is a form of grace that helps you to recognize and relinquish your projections and preconceptions.

When the topic of Guru comes up, the knee-jerk reaction of many contemporary people is to launch into stories of Gurus gone wrong. Many of these stories involve the sexual escapades of teachers. Such stories are largely based on preconceptions about spirituality in general and Tantra in particular.

Sometimes the first question a new student will ask is about Gurus-gone-wrong. There is a challenging, "I dare you" tone to these questions. One of the most interesting things about the preoccupation with faulty Gurus is that it keeps some people thinking about Gurus! Actually, such students secretly wish to be relieved of the burden of their skepticism. They are upset because they have a longing, even if unrecognized, to discover the teacher in whom they can take refuge.

Tantra is a householder tradition. This means that, since ancient times and continuing today, Tantrik Gurus have lived outside of ashrams and have married and raised families. In addition, both Indian and Tibetan forms of Tantra can involve doing sexual sadhana. This can be done as internal ritual, but the ritual is also (less frequently) performed externally with a partner. That partner might be a Guru.

The existence of sexual sadhana has always invited misunderstanding and abuse. Even in the ancient Tantras, you can read complaints about unscrupulous people calling themselves Gurus in order to lure women into having sex with them.

Despite this, no one who has entered into an authentic Guru-disciple relationship with a Tantrik Guru should be cultivating outrage, hurt feelings or resentment about their teacher's sexual or other activities. If you do find that you are cultivating these kinds of habitual reactions, you must take responsibility for that reactivity and make your reactivity part of your sadhana. Taking responsibility means that once you become aware of the reactive patterns you have inherited or collected along the way, you then make the effort to relax them.

Put your energy into your own realization rather than into reforming or criticizing teachers.

Very few highly realized teachers live on the Earth at any one time. Even teachers with a great deal of accomplishment are still to some degree a mixed bag. If we all had to wait around for totally realized teachers, this would be a sorry world indeed.

The wonderful thing is that the Guru function works effectively through teachers who have only some degree of realization. To whatever degree a teacher can recognize and embody unlimited Shiva nature, it is being made available for the student to experience. As long as both teacher and student have a solid core of sincere and unstoppable desire for discovering Reality, lack of total realization need not hinder anyone. The way in which the teacher shows up, warts and all, still functions as a mirror and gateway for the student who can take responsibility and bring all of her reactivity into the path.

Of course, most students leave a teacher or two during the course of a lifetime. Anandamayi Ma had this to say about changing teachers:

> *It suffices to receive from a person whatever little bit one is destined to receive from him. Incidents take place according to that. Also, after taking initiation from a Guru, one may feel repentant afterwards; one may not like it anymore - that is also possible. In that situation it is said that whatever little bit the disciple was destined to receive from the Guru, he has got just that much. There is something more, - you first hire a horse cart to catch the train; after you have got inside the train, you should not belittle the horse-carriage,*

*for it is the horse-carriage that has taken you to the
railway station.* (*Ananda Varta* 34.1: 8)

Of course, sometimes delusions, rather than relaxation, can build
up on both sides. But from the perspective of a sincere student,
whether your teacher is a *siddha* or sleaze ball, or anything in between, the situations are identical in this respect: Your reactivity is
still your reactivity. Taking responsibility for your reactivity, expanding your View and developing greater discrimination might lead to
you stay with a teacher, or it might prompt to you leave. But whether you stay or go, doing either out of fear and reactivity will cause
you to lose the growth potential inherent in any situation.

*Looking at your real situation is painful. Breaking habits of shame
and blame is hard. Being totally responsible is the key.*

Most people just don't want to give up their beliefs, convictions,
self-definitions, habitual reactions and compulsive pleasures. They
certainly don't want a Tantrik Guru messing up their plans and arrangements! We are all tending in the direction of *moksha* (liberation), but some of us would rather just keep on "tending." There is
absolutely nothing wrong with this.

The desire to embark fully on the Tantrik path is a matter of fate,
that huge constellation of unknowable events that burps out a full-
on Tantrika now and then. Our only job is to live authentically and
responsibly. No shame. No blame.

SEDUCING THE GURU

The joke is, we carry on about teachers who seduce their students when nearly every student is constantly trying to seduce the teacher.

How do students seduce the teacher? In the "right" hands, any of the following forms of conduct can be used for purposes of seduction.

Displaying a lot of knowledge.

Displaying charming ignorance.

Asking interesting questions.

Waiting patiently.

Waving the banner of our courage.

Waving the banner of our anger.

Waving the banner of our sincerity.

Waving the banner of our "correct" View.

Waving the banner of our desperation.

Waving the banner of our devotion.

Waving the banner of our spiritual accomplishments.

Waving the banner of our humility.

Joking around.

Seriousness.

Listening to the teacher a certain way.

Looking at the teacher a certain way.

Dressing a certain way.

Dressing to look as if we don't care how we dress.

Favors and service rendered to the teacher, the teacher's family, or the teacher's top students.

Anything we do to be number one.

Serving humbly as number two with the intent of proving we are superior to number one.

Gossiping to the teacher about other students.

Ostentatiously giving money to the teacher.

Secretly giving money to the teacher.

Flirting with the teacher.

Sex.

Challenging with criticism.

Challenging with difficult "problems."

Challenging with the teachings of other teachers.

Ostentatiously doing spiritual practice in public gatherings where the teacher is present.

Wowing the teacher with amazing dreams.

Wowing the teacher with amazing experiences.

Wowing the teacher with amazing coincidences.

Lying to the teacher.

Rejecting the teacher, but not going away.

Leaving and coming back repeatedly.

Outrageous conduct.

Perfect conduct.

Dissolute conduct.

Anything we do to be noticed.

Anything we do to be noticed not needing to be noticed.

When you try to seduce the teacher, you make the teacher ordinary. You are asking the teacher to support your fixations instead of to assist you in relaxing them. This is what people do in just about every relationship. This is what we call "compatibility." *I'll support your fixations if you support mine.*

The important thing is to notice, over time, all the ways in which you are trying to seduce the teacher. Every time a seduction works, you feel a little pleasure, but that is just small I getting its fix. This repeated, limited pleasuring reinforces dualistic vision. Karmic momentum gathers strength in the direction of nonfreedom. You will always need another shot of seduction.

When you catch yourself in the act of seduction, recognize that this is just a pattern and relax. In each moment, you can throw off your habit pattern like shrugging off a jacket or shawl. At first, the karmic pattern doesn't stay "off" for very long. But over time, the moments of relaxing add up, and the pattern can resolve naturally.

Great teachers instantly recognize efforts to seduce them and do all sorts of discomforting things to make students become more self-aware. Nobody enjoys this crash course in learning about their fixations, which is why more people are not on the direct path! But as Tantrik practitioners, we appreciate the grace that, in this life, we have such opportunity. And by tasting relaxation over and over again, we come to understand how we can work with our fixations and also that they, too, are expressions of the infinite expressive potential of God.

TANTRIK TANTRUM

A student told me a story about a teacher who expressed disappointment in his students. They weren't good enough for him. My teachers, on the other hand, generally did their best to make us students as "bad" as possible.

The head of my lineage, Paramahamsa Satyananda Saraswati, described his method of working with students this way: *I don't give them anything they want, and I give them everything they don't want.* Then he giggled (Eugene, DVD).

This is a recipe for a Tantrik tantrum! When you are not getting what you want, and you are simultaneously getting what you don't want, the force of your attachments in the form of preferences and aversions becomes naked and strong. In this situation, you cannot avoid learning about your fixations.

Only when we learn about our fixations can we work to relax them using the teachings. What we don't recognize can and will limit us.

My diksha Guru held retreats that lasted for weeks. Students arose at 4 am and worked or practiced continuously until 9 pm or later. No days off. You can bet that there were a bunch of Tantrik tantrums being thrown at these shindigs!

People acted out their fixations for all to see and experience. It could get pretty uncomfortable. But we understood clearly that any reactivity we experienced to how someone else showed up in the world was just that: *our reactivity*. No one else's responsibility.

In the end, if you were working your practice, taking responsibility and relaxing with what actually is, you discovered empathy and compassion, even for the student you wanted to strangle at the beginning of the retreat. And for yourself.

My teachers would do anything possible to bring awareness of fixations to students and to give us the tools to help us relax and expand our way of being in the world. I've gotten hard sadhana, hugs and a variety of "hits."

When you ask someone to teach you in a Tantrik tradition, expect anything. Expect that your teacher wants you to Self-realize and will do anything to help bring that about.

Fixations plus the natural desire to self-realize are the tools we have to work with in Tantra. We always work with exactly what we've already got and with exactly what shows up. If you are a student, recognize that getting naked in a Tantrik tradition does not mean taking off your clothes and hopping into a candlelit bathtub with your partner. It means recognizing your real situation and working directly with that.

Students who try to hide their fixations from teachers only reveal another layer of fixation. So, the first thing that any student of authentic Tantra might want to consider is surrendering or dropping any sense of embarrassment.

Being human is absolutely not embarrassing. Embarrassment and shame are not your inner dimension. They are just the outer controls, the containers for your real life. Let go, and your real life can begin.

THE ONLY NICE GURU IS A DEAD GURU

Lots of people claim dead Gurus as their root or Satguru. Swami Sivananda of Rishikesh, Ramana Maharshi, Anandamayi Ma, Ramakrishna and Neem Karoli Baba are favorites of the dead Guru set. This is somewhat of a tradition, and it seems to be even more prevalent in India.

Add to this the more recent phenomenon of the world-itinerant Guru. Many teachers now travel incessantly around the globe, hitting each location for only a day or two. A student might see her Guru only once a year, or even less frequently. Just enough time to get a bit of instruction. During the other 364 days, one is free to dream up feel-good fantasies.

By and large, people with dead or absent Gurus are in greater danger of remaining wrapped up in the illusion and delusion that preserves small I's sense of separation and feeds karmic habit patterns.

How can you discern if this is your situation? If your dead Guru never scares you, confuses you, pisses you off, makes you cry with frustration or electrifies you with self-recognition, you are not in a Satguru relationship.

Dead or alive, near or far, a true Guru is a mirror of unconditional openness in which you can clearly, and terrifyingly, see the degree to which you are caught up in the tensions of "me, myself and I."

Even the open flow of compassion through your Guru should come with a hint of the terrifying. Why? Because the oceanic compassion of a Satguru sweeps away all concepts, all safe bunkers of self-limiting ideas. No more Hallmark versions of love, or New Age self-serving "bliss." The Satguru shows us what is possible in the context of a human life, and it is so much more than anything we can imagine.

The Satguru answers our longing so fully, we discover the cosmic nature of that longing. You might cry like a baby upon hearing Reality's answer to its little child, but it will be a cry so simple and complex, so complete and inadequate, so full of wonder, relief, and despair, so utterly paradoxical, there will be no way to tell stories about it later on.

If, in your relationship with your dead Guru, you are always in a state of nice, comfortable, blissed-out bhakti, or ordinary and equally comfortable rationalization, you can be sure that a healthy dose of self-delusion is still at play. A person who functions as a real Satguru for us rips open our hearts so we can discover the limitless heart of Shiva nature.

The Satguru's compassion is both tender and fierce. Not knowing the fierce aspect of compassion means, for most of us, that we will not find the strength to recognize our real condition.

The Satguru's compassion is utterly personal and utterly impartial. It exactly meets our unique situation, yet flows equally for all. For this reason, a Satguru can never be bargained with, or seduced.

Not recognizing, or knowing the impartial aspect of compassion means that we will not open to unconditional compassion. Our expression of compassion will remain limited and self-motivated.

Discovering the Satguru, meeting the opportunity of Satguru, is discovering the ineffable something for which you have always longed but could never name. You may want to throw yourself at your Guru's feet, fall into your Guru's arms, and run away all at the same time.

Whatever your Guru says or does, and whatever your reaction, even in the midst of seeming to reject what your teacher is showing you, you will know without a doubt that you are being delivered to the truth of your situation.

The Satguru is an explosion of Reality in your body, your mind and your heart.

This explosion may be noisy and dramatic, or nearly imperceptible. But nonetheless, it is a situation of tremendous dynamism. You find yourself deeply moved. You cannot help but tremble at times with both fear and relief.

A teacher is chosen after due consideration. You do not choose a Satguru. Satguru is not a decision. Satguru is a sudden discovery of your Self.

The world presents us with infinite possibilities for Self-realization. So, why not a dead Guru, or far-away Guru? If a student is capable of meeting the ever-present phenomenon of Satguru in this form, why not?

Satguru operates irrespective of space and time. Satguru is focalized through a human being, but it is not contained by that human being. However, recognize that to meet Reality in the mirror of a Guru who is no longer in a human body and sharing our everyday lives requires tremendous determination, longing for Reality and discernment.

A friend of mine who is a direct disciple of Anandamayi Ma's told me that he feels it is easier for those disciples who never met her because they do not have to encounter the Guru's personality. They only perceive her "pure" form. This is a misunderstanding. Human personality is also an expression of Shiva nature. Dealing with your reactions to the Guru's personality is an important part of your sadhana.

Guru's function is to aid us in seeing ourselves with total clarity. We see both our full potential and our reactivity reflected in the mirror of Guru. A fantasy relationship cannot do this work for us. Most of us need the phenomenon of Guru in our lives, up close and personal, showing us the way.

WHERE'S MY GURU?

Anandamayi Ma said that people can pass by great beings and never know it. Others travel thousands of miles to meet a Guru and receive everything they need to awaken within a few moments. Still others unexpectedly meet Guru and find that their entire lives irrevocably turn in a new direction. Most of us remain as disciples of our Gurus for many years, if not lifetimes.

Meeting any true Guru, recognizing that encounter and being able to take a certain amount of nourishment from it means that you have cultivated the conditions for this to occur, either in this life, or a previous life. Cultivation means your own effort to wake up from the slumber we call normal human existence.

You have made the effort to recognize your desire to know yourself and your world, and you have cultivated that to a certain degree.

A person who has not yet made this effort may hear of a teacher and think: *Oh, that sounds interesting*, but they have not cultivated enough Self-recognition, or desire to Self-recognize. And so they will not go to meet the teacher.

Maybe the teacher is 1,000 miles away, or 100 or only a few, but that won't matter. Something will always seem to be in the way. *I don't have the money, or the time. It's raining outside. I'm tired. I can't find a babysitter. My partner won't like it. I already have plans.* A reasonable sounding reason will always take precedence.

Or maybe someone meets a good teacher, but the teacher does not match up with the person's concept of what a teacher is supposed to be and how a teacher is supposed to act. The person feels a little uncomfortable around the teacher and automatically thinks something is wrong because of that. Many people assume that they should only feel happiness when they are around spiritual teachers and when they do spiritual practice.

All this means is that someone is not ready for Guru. A person who is ready will be aware, to some degree, that it is her own concepts about herself and her world that are causing her to suffer, and she will be open to having these challenged. This person will go to meet the teacher no matter what and will show up ready to learn and be transformed.

Thousands of people met Anandamayi Ma and benefited from being in her presence, but she was Guru to only a relatively small number of these. This is also true of the teachers who travel around today and have thousands of devotees. It's actually much easier these days to meet a great teacher than it was years ago, but just meeting a great teacher does not mean that you have met your Guru.

Meeting your Guru is a total cosmic situation. You are meeting your own Self reflected to you by another in a special way that you can recognize. A person has to be ready for this to occur.

Who is ready for every cherished self-concept and limitation to be pointed out, shown up for what it really is and relentlessly hunted down? Only those whose natural desire to Self-realize has begun to reveal itself as the Shakti that plays in all forms of life.

So, the short answer to the question "Where is my Guru?" is another question. *Where are you?* What are you really willing to do to receive teachings? Are you ready to let go and play along?

SURRENDER AND SATGURU

To have a teacher is an immense blessing. To discover Satguru is immeasurable grace.

And yet, even having discovered Satguru, there can be arguments, criticisms, fears, and doubts. Paramahamsa Satyananda Saraswati once became so angry with his Guru, Swami Sivananda of Rishikesh, he locked himself in his room and refused to come out for two days. This was ostensibly because his Guru insisted on feeding some late night guests after the ashram kitchen was supposed to be closed.

Anandamayi Ma had a disciple who often expressed anger toward Ma. Ma said that an angry disciple was constantly thinking of her and that this would be of benefit in the end.

What is the difference between the criticisms and negative emotions we cultivate in everyday life and those that arise in the company of a Satguru?

There is no difference. Our limitations are our limitations. However, in the presence of Satguru, everything that arises more readily reveals itself as a vehicle for realization.

The Satguru's function is to continually give the disciple a taste of unconditioned Reality.

For instance, if I am floating in a swimming pool inside of a building, I am having a different experience than if I am floating in the very same swimming pool under the open sky overlooking a vast ocean. In the second situation, I notice the limitation of the swimming pool more easily. Satguru is the sky and the ocean.

Under the influence of the vast, oceanic presence of Satguru, we find it harder to convince ourselves that it is worth remaining imprisoned in our concepts and compulsions. We are more likely to bring these into our practice, take responsibility for them, work with the and let them go. We are more likely to surrender the deathly grip of "me, myself, and I" because now we have a glimpse of our real inheritance.

Many people have trouble with the whole idea of surrender. We are trained to think of ourselves as victims, or as always in danger of being victimized. We are always on guard, protecting our "boundaries" and our "independence."

But the state of the world is continuity. We are having an experience of being individual. The experience is real, but our condition is continuity. The only "individual" here is an infinite Self. We have no boundaries. The psychological ego that some of us so strongly guard has no independent existence. It is a historical and experiential blip on the screen.

When we surrender to Guru, we are really surrendering our fixations and taking refuge in our real condition of continuity with all life. Only after surrendering small I's defensiveness can we discover the natural independence of Shiva nature.

Satguru continually creates opportunities for us to taste our real condition of continuity and relax into that. This is the actual meaning of surrender.

Satguru, while usually appearing to us in the form of a teacher, in truth permeates all life with the light of primordial compassion and intelligence. Recognizing this, there is no impulse to declare one's independence by criticizing others, or by proclaiming one's superior accomplishment, beliefs, realization or understanding.

Eventually, all of these "pleasures" surrender themselves in the vastness of Satguru, like petals of flowers voluntarily offering themselves at the feet of the world.

HOW TO FIND A TANTRIK GURU

If you have done even a little bit of exploration of an authentic Tantrik tradition, you know that the Guru-disciple relationship is the central practice. Yes, we work with mantra and yantra. We practice kriya yoga and Ayurvedic self-care. We do dream practice, mind training and nonconceptual meditation. But the heart of everything is Guru.

You work with the teacher to awaken within yourself a memory of the natural state. Then you use your practices to develop your connection to that transmission and make it your own home.

Most of us need a teacher who has walked the path before us and can guide us. Otherwise, we may take long detours, or fall into a ditch of fixation masquerading as real understanding. But how can we find a good teacher? This is a question I am asked more than any other.

Realize that the circumstance of finding an authentic teacher is a response to your activity. There will also be past-life karmas at work. Everything in this manifest world is participating in a grand conversation. If you are not speaking intelligibly, no one can respond.

If you want to join the conversation and receive a response, you must develop these "languages": longing for a teacher, sincerity of purpose, courage and persistence.

My own path is instructive. I started "falling into" situations with teachers at the age of fifteen. I was unaware of any spiritual leanings, but things kept happening. This is grace and past-life karma at work.

Each time a teacher came along, I had to take some bold action outside of my comfort zone in order to accept those teachings. This was my part. You have to grab at opportunities. The world is generous. Many opportunities arise, but if you don't grab them, you will have to wait.

Finally, when I became aware that I was indeed on a spiritual path, I began to explore and develop that with great persistence, every day. I had plenty of fixations to work with, one of which was anxiety about traveling. This often is a great hindrance if you want teachings and a teacher.

Many people write to me that they want a teacher, but that there is no Tantrik Guru in their little town somewhere out in the countryside! They feel that this is a credible obstacle. I sympathize with this limited vision, but it has to be gotten over by developing such a driving desire to find a teacher that it overcomes all other considerations.

You might want to read some of the many stories about the efforts other students make to receive teachings. This will put things into perspective. It is unlikely that you will have to build and tear down and build again dozens of stone houses, as did Milarepa before his teacher would acknowledge him. But you likely will have to make some effort that you now consider to be "too much," "impossible" or outside of your normal frame of reference.

After many years of cultivating understanding, sincerity of purpose, my daily practice and longing for a lineage teacher, finally I made the move that brought me to my *diksha* (initiation) Guru. Again, this circumstance came about through a combination of seen and unseen factors, but I definitely had my part to play.

Surrendering to my Satguru years later also took great effort and courage on my part and a great showering of grace on Hers. Who knows what else? The factors are infinite. For each person, the path is a totally unique combination of matured desire, bold action and grace.

Not everyone who thinks they want a Tantrik Guru will find one in this lifetime. But Reality has only one aim: Self-realization. Whatever happens is in service to that aim. If you can look at every circumstance of your life this way, even the very painful stuff, and work with it as a practitioner, eventually your sincerity and sense of purpose will win the day.

In the meantime, grab at opportunities to sit in satsang with good teachers. Study and explore. Develop your desire and consistency of intention. When opportunity arises, notice the fixations that keep you from grabbing at it, and see if just might be your moment to step boldly onto the path of greater freedom.

SADHANA DIARIES

Coming and going, the thing is accomplished.
—*Sri Anandamayi Ma*

REMEMBERING AND FORGETTING

S PIRITUAL PRACTITIONERS QUICKLY learn that their unfoldment progresses in a pulse-like manner. If we are working hard, we go through times in which all of our obscurations, confusions and tensions come out to play. At other times, we are the embodiment of equanimity. Experiences of joy, confusion, doubt and clarity, of gratitude and upsetness with God move through us like waves that meet the shore and then recede back into the sea.

Noticing the coming and going of a more relaxed way of being in the world is the first step on the path of recognition and remembrance. The word for Self recognition in direct realization Tantra is *pratyabhijña* (prat-yuh-BHIG-nyuh). Pratyabhijña means to recognize yourself, and eventually everything and all phenomena, as the Supreme Self.

Flashes of Self recognition come and go as we work with our teachers and practice. But by continually pausing to savor the moments of greater relaxation, we get the "taste" of moksha. We try our best to remember and remain in that condition.

Many teachers have spoken eloquently about this as a process of stringing the moments of greater relaxation together like pearls until you have a whole necklace.

The pulsation we experience in our sadhana is an instance of the pulsation of the entire cosmic process, just writ a little smaller. Shiva nature continually produces experiences of greater and lesser contraction and expansion, or condensation and subtilization. Another way of understanding the pulsation is as a natural movement between experiences of greater understanding and embodiment of enlightened Shiva nature and experiences of relative ignorance and limitation.

Across the entire field of experiencing, Shiva and Shakti, in their myriad forms of appearing, continually enjoy experiencing each other as two and then rediscovering each other as one again. Shakti is "stolen" from Shiva when only duality is recognized and nonduality forgotten. She rejoins her consort when remembrance of the real nature of Self is accomplished.

When we remember our essence nature, we feel ease, spaciousness and delight. When we forget, we feel tense and alone. Through the pulsing comings and goings experienced during the course of sadhana, we eventually dance "backwards" to rediscover the Lord.

THE SANDHI

Pronounced sund-hee, the *sandhi* is a nondimensional "space" of infinite potentiality, a dynamic gap where one thing is becoming another, but has not quite arrived. For this reason, the sandhi can be described as a juncture between the manifest and the unmanifest. Living from within the creative spaciousness of infinite potentiality is the fruit of all direct realization practice.

Tantrikas explore and meditate on various sandhi in order to get a taste of the fundamental openness of Reality. Some of these sandhi are:

❖ The sandhi between day and night.
❖ The sandhi between inhalation and exhalation.
❖ The sandhi between one thought and another.
❖ The sandhi between one mantra repetition and another.
❖ The sandhi between closely fitting objects, for instance between your body lying on the floor and the floor, or between your closed upper and lower eyelids.
❖ The chakras—the sandhi from which you come into manifestation.
❖ The sandhi of *sushumna nadi*, your central, or "middle" channel.

Tantrikas try to practice at the sandhi times of day and the sandhi of each year (solstices). Kriya yoga consists of internal work with sandhi through the use of breath, visualization and movement.

Sandhi are zones of spaciousness, dynamic stillness, vitality, potential becoming and potential unbecoming.

Imagine yourself riding a large Ferris wheel. The wheel turns inexorably, moving you to the apex of your circuit. In one moment, the upward movement is slipping out of being, while downward movement is slipping into being, but nothing has definitively completed or begun. At the top of the wheel, there is a feeling of suspension, of a gap or of greater spaciousness.

We can all sense this. We feel dynamically suspended in the middle of a pause that cannot really be a pause because the wheel has not stopped turning. Yet, the Ferris wheel sandhi has duration, texture, pregnancy, spaciousness and an indefinable specialness. We all wait for that very moment. It is almost the reason why Ferris wheels exist.

The effects of the sandhi are not illusory, or unreal. They are our human way of recognizing—literally remembering—the unnamable, indescribable reservoir of unconditioned life from which all forms of manifestation emerge. Thus, the sandhi is the gateway to experiencing the most fundamental Reality.

Whatever manifest life and death are, they become tangible as the result of their emergence and subsidence. This experience of continual passage implies that every moment is a sandhi, or inbetween. (Tibetan Buddhist teachers use the word "bardo.") It's like in those science fiction movies where people move from one world to another through a kind of silvery liquid diaphragm.

A typical scene in this kind of science fiction features someone getting stuck inside the portal between worlds, or states of existence. While from the outside, the diaphragm looks nearly two dimensional, the person stuck within finds a space of infinite dimension.

Where do you think we got this idea? From our own experience, even if largely unrecognized by us!

HOW TO PRONOUNCE A MANTRA

Mantras are the subtle chemical catalysts of the cosmos. They have effects in the world. They are embodied, creative, active wisdom. When we do mantra practice, called *"japa"* in Sanskrit, we are trying to directly realize and embody the wisdom of the mantra.

For a mantra to be "incorrect" means that it is dysfunctional; it does not have *vidya Shakti,* or wisdom energy. An incorrect mantra is not actually a mantra. It is just a word, or bunch of words.

There are three answers to the question of pronunciation.

Some mantras are universal mantras in that they may be practiced with good result by anyone, even if you do not have mantra initiation. These are mantras such as *Om, Om Namo Narayani, Om Namo Narayana, Om Nama Shivaya* and *Om Ma.*

If you are practicing one of these mantras without the guidance of a teacher, you should do your best to learn the correct pronunciation. You can ask a person who knows Sanskrit, or try to find a reliable recording on the Internet. I would not recommend learning these mantras, or any mantra, from a kirtan recording. Mantras sung in kirtan have a different intonation than the same mantra used for japa practice. Also, Western kirtan singers often mispronounce mantras.

The best way to get a mantra is to receive it from a teacher who has realized the wisdom of the mantra. Realizing the wisdom of the mantra is called "piercing" the mantra. If a teacher has pierced the mantra, then she will be able to transmit the mantra to you in an activated form. This means, instead of starting from step one, you will be starting your practice from step ten. The teacher takes the "lid" off of the mantra through her or his own practice and then gives it to you.

If you receive a mantra from a teacher via initiation, you should practice the mantra exactly as it is given to you.

Even if the pronunciation is different from what you have heard elsewhere, you should do it as your teacher instructs. The mantra your teacher gives you is the form of the mantra he has realized, not some other sound.

One time, a teacher of mine transmitted a very powerful healing mantra. It was in Sanskrit, but the words were pronounced very differently from how I have been taught to pronounce them. I had to record my teacher chanting the mantra so that I could learn his pronunciation exactly and unlearn the "correct" pronunciation.

Later, I heard that the teacher was angry because some people had complained about his pronunciation! Later, he gave the mantra again in perfect university Sanskrit. I always suspected that this was not the real mantra.

Another answer about how to pronounce a mantra is illustrated by this story. A certain person had been a yogi in a former life, but in order to resolve some karma, in his present life he was a simple, uneducated farmer.

One day, the farmer heard monks chanting a mantra. It was a mantra the farmer had practiced a lot in his former life, but of course he didn't remember this now. However, he felt attracted to the mantra, so he started to chant it as best he could, pronouncing it in some funny way.

Day after day, plowing up and down his fields, the farmer constantly chanted the mantra. As years went by, the farmer and his family prospered. The farmer became more and more peaceful and expansive in his view. Although he was uneducated in this life, he began to directly remember some of the wisdoms he had previously learned, and so he became a respected person in his community.

One day, a scholar walked by the farm and heard the farmer chanting the mantra as he plowed his field. The scholar addressed the farmer saying: *You are pronouncing that mantra incorrectly, you ignoramus!* The farmer felt very bad about this. He begged the scholar to teach him the correct pronunciation. This made the scholar feel important, which he liked. And so he gave the farmer the corrected mantra.

More time went by, and the farmer's life again had changed, but this time for the worse. His crops were failing. He and his family became poor, and the farmer no longer gave such wise advice to his neighbors.

Now the scholar happened to come by again. He heard the farmer, doggedly repeating the "correct" mantra, and he saw the conditions of the farmer's life had changed. He realized his mistake and immediately asked the farmer to go back to his old way of pronouncing. The farmer happily did so, and his life prospered again.

This story illustrates that when fate, grace, diligence and devotion align in a person's life, all bets are off; anything can be accomplished.

SPIRITUAL EXPERIENCES: FACT OR FICTION?

One of the most useful pieces of advice about spiritual experiences I received is this: *Throw out everything and see what's left.*

Seems like a simple statement, right? But when you investigate further, it's rather enigmatic. What does it mean to "throw out everything?" And what is left when you do so?

Here's what I've learned.

First things you should throw out, of course, are those experiences you've made up, exaggerated, embellished over time or elevated beyond reason. These include random shadows and flashes; hokey "coincidences"; candles "mysteriously" blowing out or similarly silly stuff; wishful thinking; vaguely spiritual dreams; contrived visions (You read it in a book and now its happening to you!); average, everyday psychic intuitions; and outright lies.

If you even suspect your "spiritual experience" falls into one or more of the categories above, be vigilant! Err on the side of caution, and toss it in the round file (the trash can). Stop talking about it, analyzing it or attaching any importance to it.

Some of these kinds of events may relate to your practice, or not. They may derive from realms other than human, or not. They may be indications of past and future lives, or not. Whatever. They are of little significance within the larger context of Self-realization.

Remember: Embody, don't embalm!

Real spiritual experiences always have some actual wisdom to convey. But instead of working to create the conditions that will turn a spiritual experience into a new basis for living, we often take that little experience into our psychic workshop and begin the lengthy embalming process. We "fatten up" the experience with spiritual aura. Then we shape it into a coherent story. We graft on the super-spiritual meaning so everyone gets how special we are. Finally, we embed the entire apparatus into a block of ego plastic so we can carry it around and drag it out at parties and spiritual gatherings.

By the time we're done with this, the wisdom is lost, and all we've got is another self-image formation. The opposite of wisdom.

When you are capable of opening to an authentic and significant spiritual transmission, whether it be from a live teacher, a dream, a vision, a flash of insight or a life circumstance, you will notice that it is not available to your usual activities of making stories and analyzing.

When you have received a wisdom transmission, you can try lobbing some analysis at it, but your attempts will bounce away like rubber balls hitting a wall. Authentic and significant spiritual transmission (wisdom experience) has a quality of imperviousness. You can feel it. When an experience can't be explained, believed, disbelieved, analyzed, narrated or even thought about in your usual ways, there is something of value being transmitted.

Far from being fodder for an overactive self-image forming mechanism, real spiritual experiences are often rejected by the everyday mind. But "deeper" than this rationalism and drive for coherency is a shift in our form of life: in how we feel, what we know and our capacity for kindness and contentment. This is what is "left" when we throw out everything else.

Wisdom conveyed through spiritual experience is a live thing. It has its own intelligence and life process. It has real effects on our View and conduct. Our attempts to make the experience into a story, or to understood it in conventional ways, generally kills our ability to make good use of the transmission.

So, if you've got some polished up spiritual experience story you've been lugging around, you can be sure it no longer contains the active principle. You've got the snake skin, but the snake got away.

Authentic spiritual experiences are not endings; they are beginnings. Spiritual experiences are work orders. You receive a "hit" of a more expanded way of being in the world. Now you have to do the work to stabilize that experience and integrate it into your life permanently.

SPIRITUAL OPPORTUNITY

Everything that happens here in the manifest world is a communication that has the potential to help us wake up and discover our real nature. When we happen to notice one of these communications, we call it a coincidence, an omen, synchronicity or a special moment of grace.

But the truth is, Lord Shiva, our own Self, is continuously showering us with grace. We just don't always recognize it. Our karmic conditioning acts like a strange drug that keeps us from acknowledging, or receiving what we are being offered.

While you are living in time, you are subject to cause and effect. Even if you are doing sadhana and are waking up, you lack total clarity. You are bound to miss some opportunities because your senses, including your mind, are still conditioned.

A great teacher announces an upcoming teaching. You want to go, but all sorts of fears arise.

You are afraid to ask for time off at work. You are worried about money. Your friend or partner wants you to do something else at the time of the teaching, and you don't want to disappoint. You think the teaching is too far, too long, too late or too early. Or you are too tired. Or you are nervous about being with a new spiritual community. Infinite obstacles can arise. These are nothing more or less than lack of clear seeing as a result of karmic conditioning.

Karma is a real force. It is consciousness and energy repeating a pattern with momentum in time. Karmic patterns repeat without regard for the uniqueness of each moment. Whether pleasant or unpleasant patterning, karmically bound activities always miss a beat, or two. There is *always* something limiting about karma.

In order to begin to release ourselves from karmic conditioning, we must achieve a certain level of clarity about our real situation.

We must be able to recognize when we are being dragged off by karmic momentum.

Karmic momentum comes with a certain compulsive, anxious-feeling texture. Even if we are tumbling along in a pleasurable pattern, we can recognize this feeling of attachment. It is not so hard. Once you train yourself to recognize, you can begin to choose differently. That's the hard part!

Even if you can't see or feel clearly what is happening, you can take advantage of the insights of your teachers, friends, family and fellow practitioners. Use everything at your disposal as a mirror.

Engaging in more appropriate movement in the face of karmic momentum is effortful. Yet it is the kind of effort that eventually frees us of karma so that we can experience *kriya*.

Kriya is spontaneous, unbound activity. Kriya is activity that is perfectly in tune with nature and does not reinforce karma. Karma promotes more tension and compulsion. Kriya is effortlessness.

For instance, kriya yoga is a system of sadhana that works with the natural flow of the subtle breath, or *prana*, in channels (*nadis*) and chakras. We learn to enter into and participate with the spontaneous movements of the subtle body. This helps us to move from karma, or bound activity, to experiencing true spontaneity.

We all pass up opportunities for growth. We don't do our practice with consistency. We miss teachings. Or perhaps we experience certain spiritual openings, and then we don't do the work to make these our home base.

When I was at a certain stage of sadhana, when I felt even the slightest tingle of awakening energy, I would stop what I was doing and would sit to do practice. Now I am more aware—both of the opportunities and of how many times, out of sheer karmic momentum, I choose to let them pass by!

In order to receive the abundance that is our constant inheritance, we must work to increase our capacity to receive. This is upsetting because those who feel lack of opportunity and nourishment do not generally want to open up to receive what they fear is not there. Why be vulnerable and put oneself in line for yet more disappointment and sadness?

You can stockpile a little more courage and confidence in the world by looking honestly at the gifts you have already been given and cultivating gratitude. The gift that always gives me more confidence is the gift of being on this path. What more could I ask for? Guru yoga is also a profound source of nourishment.

THE WHOOMPH FACTOR

When we feel sadness, or frustration or pain, then we feel badly about these feelings. We think we are supposed to feel better. So we feel pain, and then we feel ashamed of our pain. And then we concoct all sorts of activities or thought remedies to try to numb the pain and the shame of pain.

When we feel happy, or in one moment, our life seems to have meaning and importance, we feel we want to prolong this state. Lurking in the background is the knowledge that we surely won't be able to prolong it, but we think we should be able to if we could just get it right. So we concoct all sorts of activities and thought remedies to try to prolong "happiness" and stave off its opposite.

We are constantly on guard. We are on guard against failure and disappointment. And we are on guard *for* happiness, success and approval. We live constantly under the threat of pain and loss of happiness, or even the threat that we might realize, in one moment, that our experience of happiness is impoverished. It is not quite complete, or lasting happiness at all.

When we begin a seated practice, we carry this pervasive sense of threat with us. Engaged in the simplicity of sitting, most of us cannot help but become the anxious watcher. Are we doing it right? Are we feeling right? Are we getting the results? How fast are we getting the results compared to others? Ah… a moment of peace. I'm doing well. I'll try to preserve that good result. Uh oh, here come the bad thoughts again. I'm doomed.

We have many concepts about what seated practice is supposed to bring us: from peace and bliss to boredom and physical discomfort. Or perhaps we are doing it mostly for approval from our teacher, or some other person. Or so that we can feel good about ourselves by antidoting our sense of shame with "spiritual" behavior.

Tenzin Palmo, one of the first Western women to become a Buddhist nun, spent twelve years in retreat in a cave high up in the Himalayas. She wrote that after twelve years in solitude, there was no aspect of herself that had not made itself known to her. (Mackenzie 144)

The same process is at work when we begin a consistent, daily, seated practice. Everything that we are will show itself sooner or later.

If we are physically stiff, we will hurt. If we are anxious and afraid, we will feel restlessness and terror. If we have squashed our natural liveliness with fantasy and overstimulation, we will feel boredom. If we are angry, we will find something or someone to be angry at. If we are sad, we may be overwhelmed by sadness. If we are seeking only peace, we will surely encounter frustration and disappointment. If we desire approval and realize that we are alone, we may feel bitterness and grief. Every little noise may seem amplified and unbearable.

Many people, finding that states of peacefulness or simple relaxation come and go, decide that their practice is not "working." If they are uncomfortable, either physically or emotionally, they feel a sense of failure, perhaps even abandoning their practice because it didn't immediately bring the good feelings they expected. They cannot sustain a seated practice because of these limiting concepts, and because the fear of naked self-encounter is too great.

Seated practice is a time and space given for us to encounter life expressing itself in all of its richness. Here, we can meet ourselves as we really are. We can begin to notice the ways in which we have used numbing out, or frantic activity to muffle our awareness and true longing. We can also begin to experience contact with a larger sense of liveliness and awareness that holds all of us, without exception, in a compassionate, loving crucible. We can begin to relax, and eventually come to laugh at the devices and ruses we employ to escape Reality.

I call this beginning phase of practice the *whoomph*. We all need to go *whoomph*—to take our own seat in our real situation without hype or adornment. From this seat in our actual experience, we can begin to Self-realize.

As in all Tantrik practice, you are an investigator of your real situation. Try to approach whatever discomfort arises with curiosity, gratitude and discernment, but without judgment. View the emotions and sensations that arise as opportunities for greater awareness, rather than as shameful, or as obstacles.

With this in mind, you can use your discernment to take appropriate action given your real condition in that moment. You may decide to shut a window if there is excessive street noise, or alter your diet and exercise so that you can sit with greater comfort and without so much fidgeting. A stubborn, heroic attitude is no less self-judging than indulging habitual feelings of failure and inadequacy.

Everything that comes up in your seated practice is appropriate to your real situation. There is no threat, nothing outside. You need not guard against anything. You need not reject or grab onto anything. Just let it rip. Only by relaxing your reflex to grab on or push away will you enjoy the full opportunity to discover what's actually here and to find lasting contentment within that unfolding Reality.

MEDITATION SATSANG

The word "meditation" gets used to mean anything from sitting quietly, to actively visualizing, to concentration on the breath, or some object, and even to cooking and jogging.

None of these activities are meditation. But we could say that they might all eventually lead to deeper relaxation if undertaken in a certain way. For instance, cooking might be relaxing, but it could also be stressful. It depends on your orientation.

Any number of practices called meditation are techniques for calming and focusing the mind. This is important for many people. Practices that involve one-pointed concentration on images, or the breath, fall into this category. This relatively crude level of one-pointedness introduces a limited experience of quietude, and it alleviates our attachment to our habitual thoughts and emotions.

Another, somewhat subtler type of "meditation" practice, involves experiencing the base state of ordinary mind. We can experience the base from which thoughts are arising and subsiding by becoming more aware of the gap between thoughts. There are many techniques for accomplishing this. But students doing this kind of practice are still experiencing the base as something inside themselves, or as an aspect of their individual mind. So we call it "ordinary mind."

Quite often, practices that lead to discovering inner silence, or to thoughtlessness, are mistaken for high levels of realization, or even for the final aim of sadhana. The experience of spaciousness can be profound, but it is not Self-realization. Self-realization does not exclude any variety of experience, including thoughts. Self-realization is independent of any phenomena.

The real nature of meditation is the world enjoying itself without any technique, without any mediation. The world has infinite richness, infinite texture, infinite variety. The primordial intelligence contemplates its own nature: the great sourceless ocean of compassion, the play of the wisdom lights of the five elements, endless permutations of space, time and timelessness, with ceaseless curiosity.

When you enter into the contemplation of Shiva nature, simply sitting becomes the greatest adventure. At the same time, one discovers the famous "one taste" of all life: the equality of all phenomena. You discover that effortless contemplation is not generated by human individuals; it is what the entire Reality *is*.

The enjoyment of Shiva nature is not some limited mental appreciation. Nor is it an amazing experience, as we Americans like to say. There are no words that capture the state of contemplation—the essence of the world. The Tantras (written teaching texts of the tradition) often call it "delight." You can discover it in every moment, every circumstance, every breath, every cell. It is not hidden behind appearances, lurking out of sight in some transcendental realm. It is the essence of all, both the ordinary and the extraordinary.

NATURAL CONTEMPLATION

People experiencing busy mind, or anxiety sometimes say: *I should learn meditation!* But meditation is not always the most useful practice in this situation. If the mind is too busy, you may not be able to fruitfully engage in a relatively formless practice.

Students must recalibrate their systems and achieve greater balance. Then entering into the state of meditation becomes more possible.

If your mind and emotions are in turmoil, the first place you want to look for recalibration is to your food, movement and daily routine. Our thoughts and emotions are energy, or Shakti. They are very much affected by what we eat and how we live.

The process of calming down and gaining more equanimity in our basic experience is called "seating the prana." Before we can sit, our prana must sit! Prana has many meanings, but in this instance, you can think of prana as your internal winds. When your mind, body and subtle energy body channels are windy, your spiritual practice will be less fruitful.

Routine is the number one medicine for soothing and organizing internal winds.

Seating the prana is achieved by doing a hatha yoga practice that is appropriate to your constitution, by eating appropriate foods and by ritualizing your day through the Ayurvedic practice of *dinacharya*. Dinacharya means "daily conduct." It is an ancient and healthy protocol for ritualizing how you wake up and conduct yourself during the day. Consulting an Ayurvedic practitioner, or a reliable book about Ayurveda, is your first step.

If you eat, sleep, work, play and move more appropriately, you will gain much more peace of mind than you will struggling to sit and meditate before you are ready.

For many students, mantra practice is a good place to begin after the prana has calmed down a bit. Mantra japa is tangible and generally enjoyable. It engages your mind, your energy, your senses and your movement as you use a mala to count. This helps to further reorient distracted senses and recalibrate them.

I teach my students three stages of meditation. The first two stages are more active. The final stage is *sahaja* meditation, or natural meditation. This is also called nonconceptual meditation, *mahamudra* or *trekchod* in Tibetan. In the beginning and middle stages, it is important to give the senses and mind something specific to do. Slowly over time, students can let go of that.

Beyond anything we could call meditation is natural contemplation. This is equal to the natural state. It is *completely free of any meditation technique.* It is without meditating. It is not something that you do. Natural contemplation is the base state of Self-awareness from which everything arises.

A person might read what I just wrote and think: *Okay, I don't have to do anything. I can just sit.* However, this person is still thinking that some special posture, or internal attitude she adopts is meditation.

Natural contemplation is not an activity, or experience generated by the limited individual; it is the inherent *bhava*, or feeling-state of Shiva nature. When we relax deeply enough, we can just enter into this and recognize it to be our own enlightened Self.

Natural contemplation is not disturbed by being in a certain posture or not being in it. It does not depend on eyes being open or closed. As limited individuals, we adopt postures, inner techniques and attitudes that we need to help us to eventually recognize our essential nature.

We use these spiritual technologies to free ourselves from compulsion. But once we are relatively relaxed, the natural arising and subsiding of thoughts and emotions does not disturb us. We can just go on being in a state of contemplation.

SUFFERING, FEAR AND PAIN

When I first came to spiritual practice, I didn't know I was suffering. I thought I was enjoying life and just looking for more. I had a lot to learn about myself and Reality!

For instance, if you are enjoying your relationships, your job, your kids or anything else you have in your life right now, imagine that something is taken away. How will you feel?

If you are at a party, and someone you don't like arrives, do you feel tense? If your boss gets mad at you, do you freak out, or lash back? If someone dies, do you grieve for years and years? If you get sick, do you feel victimized, or scared?

This is one way of looking at human suffering. At every moment, our so-called happiness is dependent on having or not having some things and circumstances. We try very hard to hold onto the things we think will make us feel good, and we push away the things we don't like. We live in a near-constant state of defensive anxiety. Much of our life is spent trying to avoid recognizing our fear of life's openness. This is suffering.

Another way of looking at suffering is that most people are experiencing compulsion most of the time. We have to do things and have things a certain way. We define ourselves very narrowly. We experience habitual emotions, activities and reactions to life. We can't stop planning and thinking.

Once you get a little bit into a spiritual practice, you realize how much of a slave you are to your habits of body, emotion and mind. This is what happened to me. I thought I was a free-wheeling kind of person. Then I began to notice all the ways of feeling, thinking and acting over which I had surprisingly little control.

The root ignorance—our belief that we are separate individuals—is the basis for all suffering.

We are firmly convinced that we are born as individuals and that we die. So we feel cut off from our essence. We are lonely, and we are afraid of death. Our habits and compulsions are distractions from these fundamental feelings.

Suffering happens when we are attached to habits of body, energy and mind that distract or divert us from directly experiencing pain. Pain itself is not suffering; it is simply a certain quantity and quality of energy. We have to be willing to touch our pain directly if we are to live an authentic life and Self-realize.

Our fear of life is very alive. Fear is an intense form of Shakti. When we run from our fear, we are running from our own vital energy. When we run from our loneliness, we are running from authentic understanding and the possibility of experiencing open-hearted compassion for ourselves and others.

As practitioners, we have to get fully and directly in touch with our condition of feeling separate and scared. The more we do this within the context of sadhana, the more we learn about ourselves and the more determined we become to discover our real nature.

FEAR AND SPIRITUAL GROWTH

Fear is an intensely alive state. Remember a moment when you felt really terrified. Electricity races everywhere in your body. Your skin seems to bubble and then disappear as you are launched into a field of energy and space. The conceptual mind short-circuits at the same time that the world appears to your senses with shocking clarity. The immediacy can be overwhelming.

Fear delivers us to boundless, unreasonable, uncontainable, nameless life. So we are indeed afraid of fear because fear is a powerful and direct gateway to nonconceptual, supercharged openness.

Tantra is often, and often erroneously, associated with sexual acts. In fact, practices that invoke fear are much more common in the tradition. In my life as a Tantrika, I have jumped off of high walls, been buried underground and have sat in meditation in woods where wild animals roamed.

I have learned to use moments of real fear as sadhana: to bring them onto my spiritual path. You can try to do this, too.

You need to begin by understanding that anxiety and fear are not the same. Worrying is what we do to avoid the piercing quality of fear. But if you have some circumstance in your life that gives rise to real fear, for instance, if you are afraid of flying in an airplane, you can use this to help you to realize.

The first thing you want to do is consciously relax your body. This will cause the fear to race through you and will bring on a feeling of free fall. Then, you want to invoke a relatively formless, eyes-open meditation practice. The best kind of meditation is nonconceptual, or sahaja meditation. A form of meditation that involves watching your thoughts, or your breath will not work so well.

You can also chant a mantra. However, if you use a mantra in this situation, you cannot cling to it as a distraction. You are not trying to antidote the fear. This is the most important point.

Chant the mantra steadily and slowly with your eyes open. If the mantra is related to a Guru or Deity, you can have a real experience of that being, very large in space in front and slightly above you. But again, don't cling to a visualization. You have to be allowing yourself to relax into an actual feeling of being present with the teacher or Deity. Keep relaxing your body.

You will feel the energy of the fear moving around within you. It will be uncomfortable, but interesting. Just let it keep unfolding. As you continue, you will learn much about your condition. If you keep on continuing, many wonderful openings can occur.

SPIRITUAL BIRTH PAINS

Various physical aches and pains can accompany the process of spiritual unfoldment. Some of the grosser manifestations of spiritual birth pains are: bands of painful tension across the forehead, uncomfortable sensations of pressure at the third eye or at other points on the head, spiritual "flus," stabbing pains, soreness at *marma* points (like acupuncture points), irregular pulses and exhaustion.

When we are practicing consistently, we are literally making ourselves available to a rebirthing process. This birth is not metaphorical. As a result of spiritual unfoldment, our form of embodiment, our body chemistry, our perceptions and our way of moving, feeling and sensing in the world will change radically.

If you are practicing more than an hour a day, at some point you will feel ill. Try not to treat spiritual birth pains with painkillers. If the symptoms are not severe, don't take any medicine at all. Just continue your sadhana. Adjust your diet and your level of effort so that your body has the nourishment it needs and the time to recalibrate.

Your entire system is undergoing a shift, and cultivating deep relaxation is usually the best way to participate. Try to remain quiet and relatively inactive so that you can relax deeply and allow the process to complete without too much interference. However, if you are concerned about your symptoms, or if you are concerned about misinterpreting them and being in a state of fantasy, see a doctor.

I knew a practitioner who thought he was becoming enlightened, but he was really suffering from heart disease. He waiting too long to see a doctor and had a heart attack.

Always see a knowledgeable Tibetan, Chinese or Ayurvedic medicine professional before you attribute any worrisome symptoms to your spiritual practice.

During a particularly intense period of sadhana, I went to a Chinese medical doctor. He examined me, and I could tell from his expression that he was quite alarmed at my condition. However, his understanding was limited to a disease perspective. He was not able to work on any other level.

The doctor I have now is himself an accomplished spiritual practitioner. He can participate on that level and assist to help changes happen more smoothly. And he knows when to back off.

In the normal course of sadhana, nearly everyone experiences some imbalances that show up as physical discomfort. A good way to orient yourself correctly to these events is to think of how difficult it is for many people to sit in a meditation posture when they are just beginning.

But one day, even a beginner might notice that all of the pains of sitting have simply disappeared. Then, the next day the pains are back. Eventually, they go away for good. We know this is not just a matter of the muscles stretching out because the pain can disappear for periods of time even when a person is relatively new on the path.

Pain is a symptom of limitation in the physical body, the energy body and the wisdom body simultaneously. These three are differing expressions of the same body. In some moment, even a beginner may experience the relaxation of limitation. This comes and goes until relaxation has taken place and stabilized on more subtle levels.

For more aggressive, "heroic" practitioners, exhaustion can also be a signal that relaxation is occurring. Of course, most people in contemporary society are chronically exhausted. The first spiritual experience that many people have is just to notice how exhausted they really are.

When we are going through an opening, it is normal to experience a kind of seasickness. We are literally opening to wisdom, to embodied understanding. Our View is enlarging and the opening of the gates of perception can cause a temporary feeling of illness as when one is unaccustomed to travel on the open sea.

The more sudden a change in one's condition, the more likely it is that pain will occur. Careful preparation under the guidance of a skillful teacher minimizes the chance that you will experience significant pain. Practicing with correct View is the foundation.

Sick effort is that quantity of energy you are putting into your practice in order to support the limited aims of small I. It is practicing with the wrong feeling, or intention, for instance to gain admiration, approval, super health, gross pleasure, dramatic breakthroughs or special powers.

We come to spiritual practice with certain imbalances in our five elements—earth, water, fire, air and space. Our practice must be specifically tailored to address these imbalances and avoid causing real harm to ourselves. A great deal of insight, experience, and discernment is necessary. For 99.99 percent of us, a teacher is absolutely required if we hope to progress and not fall into fantasy and unnecessary encounters with health imbalances.

Several well-known published accounts of the rise of kundalini have been written by people who were apparently quite unprepared for the experience. Unfortunately, the experiences recounted in these books have been taken for the norm. As a result, many people believe these extremely uncomfortable symptoms are desirable signs of spiritual growth. They are not. They are symptoms of blockage. With the guidance of a knowledgeable teacher, many of these symptoms can be minimized or avoided altogether.

Various website discussion groups are filled with people experiencing many different kinds of illnesses that are uniformly, and in most cases, incorrectly attributed to kundalini rising. It is not out of the question that a person could die if gross disease is incorrectly attributed to spiritual practice, or if practice is done incorrectly without proper guidance.

During the course of my sadhana, I experienced some severe symptoms such as fever and heart irregularities. I am extremely grateful to my teachers for assisting me in these times, particularly for helping to have a correct View of such episodes. I needed to understand that my symptoms were the result of sick effort and were not badges of spiritual heroism, or superiority.

Practitioners sometimes become attached to uncomfortable symptoms, or just to any manifest physical sensations that arise during the course of practice. Remember that the fruit of practice is actual, usable wisdom, not just sensation. We may experience various sensations along the way as we deal with tensions and then relax, but these sensations are not the goal.

Attachment is the most pervasive pitfall for any person. Whatever you are attached to becomes an obstacle. Constantly remember this, and you are well on your way home.

FUMES, OR VAJRA PRIDE?

We human beings all encounter difficult circumstances along with feelings that our lives have crashed, emotionally and mentally. Experiences such as health crises, death of a loved one, job loss, or natural disaster can bring along with them the feeling that we no longer know who we are, or what life is all about.

Simply in the course of everyday life, you will surely experience feelings of anxiety, or disassociation. The world seems strange to you. You seem strange to yourself. Suddenly the "you" you thought you were seems as ephemeral as gasoline fumes on a hot summer's day.

Many people "treat" these episodes with the medicine of a mad scramble back to familiar habits of self-image-making. Or they use drugs to antidote the anxiety and depression triggered when the knowledge that their self-image is running on fumes rises up from the depths of their being, from the inexhaustible wellspring of life.

People generally do not have the cultural support to recognize panic, anxiety and depression as messages of wisdom, as opportunities to divest ourselves of the habits of body, energy and mind that are damaging our health and hindering our spiritual growth.

In general, we approach breakdowns large and small as if they are primary issues, when actually they are secondary to the fact that our lives are out of sync with Nature. Rather than antidoting such experiences with efforts to reconstruct a self-image, Tantrik practice is designed to *bring on* crises of self-image and self-concept.

Within the context of a loving Guru-disciple relationship and consistent sadhana, we can discover the wisdom virtues that are expressing themselves through our so-called negative emotions. We can work directly to discover vajra pride.

Vajra means diamond-like, or adamantine. It is the unshakable pride of Shiva nature in its own essence nature and all that it creates out of itself. When small I relaxes, we step out of the fumes of compulsive self-image making and experience adamantine confidence in life just as it is.

The fumes of self-image can take many shapes: I am this; I am that. My life plan. My accomplishments. The stuff I own. My house. My car. My job. My superiority. Even my inferiority. Yes, the reason why people with "inferiority complexes" have nervous breakdowns when they succeed beyond their expectations is because their self image has broken down and they experience openness for the first time.

Self-image is any story we repeatedly tell about ourselves, whether it feels good or not-so-good. We mistake this repetition for our essence nature. But it is just karmic patterning.

Fumes of any variety create a momentary feeling of enjoyment. Even complaining about ourselves is fun. We get high on fumes, so of course, when our fume-producing mechanism breaks down, we crash.

A self-image breakdown has the potential to deliver us to greater openness, possibility and spontaneity. But we have defined breakdowns as problems. Breakdowns in self-image often come with loss. Someone who served as our externalized self leaves us. We get fired from a job. We are confronted with failure.

Such breakdowns are scary. The fear of openness comes rushing in. We want to figure out who we are, again. We want to get back on the fumes as quickly as possible. But by doing so, we just sign on for another round of compulsive highs and painful lows.

The only real refuge from this cycle is to relax our tensions, our self-image-making effort, and live in open expectation. We should aim to live like a person who is welcoming to any guest that life brings her way. Our goal should be to skillfully adapt to whatever shows up, not to try to trap life and hold it under our control.

Successful adaptation does not mean that we will never experience pain or sadness. These are integral aspects of human life. But if we are not so hard at work creating a self-image, we will not be condemned to experiencing such episodes as attacks.

I had an experience of this the first time I went to India. I had big plans and a big image of myself as the great yogini going off to do "serious" practice in the Motherland. Instead, I got dengue fever, and nothing turned out the way I expected.

At some point, I relaxed (but not too quickly!), and stopped fighting the natural course of my life. I was still quite ill, but I remember that my teacher remarked on how well I looked. He said that this happens when you don't resist life's ups and downs. I felt weak but surprisingly content.

Slowly over time, I realized that everything is fine. The totality of life and everything it brings our way is unproblematic. This is the beginning of realizing vajra pride.

PROMISES AND VOWS

People in many traditions take vows. Vow-taking powerfully orients one toward the accomplishment of the vow. Vow-taking creates momentum. In some traditions, people take hundreds of vows. The keeping of vows is in fact their main practice.

Once, I was instructed in a dream not to take any more vows. My flesh and blood teacher instructed me otherwise, and that got me contemplating the whole vow phenomenon. I had a feeling back then that the only authentic vows were those that had somehow already been made, but I didn't really understand my own intuition.

Later, I experienced what might be called "vow events." These were spontaneous vows, made and accomplished simultaneously. In those moments, I recognized a few things about vows.

Vows are open communications. When we are in a state of open communication, our small sense of self has dissolved. A complete vow is like a sudden opening of the gates of the self.

A complete vow is heard. The world answers and validates it.

A complete vow is fulfilled without fail. You may backtrack a little, you may fall into temporary disgrace, but a complete vow pulls you toward wisdom inexorably. No complete vow can ever be broken or abandoned.

A complete vow is surrender to your real situation. We tend to think of taking a vow as a moment in which we pull ourselves together, get tough and buck up. However, a complete vow is as sweet and natural as water.

A complete vow is alchemy. It transforms your experience of body, energy and mind.

Ordinary promises have their place. But we all know that if a friend says: *I'll be over for dinner at 8:00*, something might get in the way—a delay or an unavoidable change in plans. We make allowances for this possibility. Maybe the friend will just forget, or decide not to be friends with us anymore. Anything can happen, even when a promise has been made.

In spiritual practice, many people conflate ordinary promises and vows. Most of us, when we say we are taking a vow, are only making an ordinary promise in fancy dress.

It is important to recognize that a spontaneous vow and a promise are different situations. A vow is not a grim affair. When we are committing to undertake some action, sometimes we sigh with tiredness at the thought of having to live up to our promise. But we experience a feeling of relaxation and joy when uttering a spontaneous vow.

> Because you are
> God becoming
> God,
> all commitments are naturally fulfilled.
> The intricate weave
> of everything-at-once
> pulls a golden thread
> and you are off!
> The only authentic vows
> are those
> that take us,
> not the vows we take
>
> When a vow comes for you,
> keep your eyes open,
> and your body relaxed
>
> Be like a newborn baby
> tossed into space

Curious and soft
no matter what

More than artificial vows,
we need this bravery
and to remember
our natural talent
for being swept away

ANGER AND SELF-REALIZATION

A student once asked me: *Do I ever have the right to be angry?*

What does "the right to be angry" mean? Basically, it means justification for continuing one's attachment to small I experiencing itself as being hurt, victimized, cheated, annoyed, frustrated and so on.

Is this what you really want? We may be stuck with our resentment and grudges temporarily because of conditioning, but as yogis, we want to end that conditioning, not insist on our "right" to become more stuck.

Who are you? And who is someone else? "You" and "other" are experiences. The other person is another expression of the experience of Self, of God. So if you reserve your right to be angry, you are only angry at God.

There is never any possibility that anyone has done us wrong. God, the Supreme Self, is communicating with total perfection. Every experience is just that.

Suffering at the hands of another can be a very powerful experience, but we do not ultimately want to be at its mercy. Think of the Tibetan Buddhist monks, who, when being tortured in Chinese prison camps, used this situation to Self-realize further.

We should try to view every situation in our lives as an opportunity to Self-realize, without shame or blame.

This is very hard. But even during the many times when we have all sorts of compulsive reactions, we should try to recognize we are in a state of compulsion and invoke our practice—our mantras, our breath, and especially Guru yoga—right then and there.

When reactivity threatens to overtake you, try to remember what you really want. Remembering the state of your Guru will make your deepest longing tangible for you. When I think of Ma, I always know right away that she is my beacon, and my reactivity is not. Remembering this, I can relax.

Anger is a beautiful expression when it is not compulsive. Self-liberating anger is like fierce, illuminating lightning. It shocks and transforms a situation instantly with its cutting-through energy.

However, self-liberating anger disappears right after the strike. It doesn't hang on, exhausting itself by continually trying to hurt and destroy. The anger that expresses through Self-realized persons leaves behind the clarity and freshness of a summer lightning storm.

SELFISHNESS AND SPIRITUAL PRACTICE

There is only one desire in this world—the desire that moves us toward Self-realization. Selfishness is that same desire expressing through a person in a state of limitation. So, instead of directly desiring Self-realization, we desire the fullness that comes from overeating, or the love of a particular person or the temporary, limited security of wealth or fame.

The many manifestations of selfishness are attempts to pleasure, protect and perpetuate the small I by a person who is suffering from feelings of separation and vulnerability.

In its less limited condition, the tension we call selfishness draws us inexorably to seek immortal consciousness and bliss. If we "act selflessly" in order to boost our self-image to get some emotional or other reward, we simply have not made a steady enough contact with the natural desire to Self-realize. That desire is still distracted or deflected toward much more limited aims.

People normally have mixed motives as they are undertaking spiritual practice. Many of these motives involve serving the compulsive desires of small I. But there is always some kernel, some seed or thread of unfettered desire to discover one's true nature. If this were not so, there would be no realization.

For instance, a person has a sincere feeling of gratitude and wants to do some karma yoga. But then they also want the work to be convenient and pleasing to themselves, and perhaps they derive gratification from being in a position of responsibility. There are mixed motives. A wise teacher uses these situations to get everyone to experience their real condition and grow.

If we continue to faithfully cultivate our practice with correct View, selfish motives, such as desires for certain kinds of spiritual accomplishments or recognition, can drive us to discover the cosmic virtues that have been embedded in our tensions all along. These virtues, the Self-ish-ness of the world Self, have other names: curiosity, compassion and devotion. When we become better conduits for these virtues, we have reached the stage at which we can begin to understand that these virtues are not the property of small I. They are a natural upsurge in the one Self experiencing itself as many.

No matter what our condition, we cannot do anything but participate in this magnificent game of waking up and discovering our real nature. "Faults" such as selfishness always contain the seeds of wisdom. Selfishness is just as natural as compassion.

Until your selfishness has blossomed to reveal the enlightened wisdom virtues of Self, you can follow the precepts laid out for you by your teachers. In this way, you can begin to participate in the play of virtue in a way is appropriate to your level of realization. You can relax within the crucible of your tradition's guidelines.

Perhaps in some years, or lifetimes, those very guidelines will reveal themselves to have been the path that led you to pathless naturalness and the spontaneous display of enlightened activity.

WORK HARD LIKE WATER

Sometimes we work hard in our sadhana with the goal of satisfying the demands of small I. These demands might take the form of compulsions to have a big "spiritual" breakthrough, to be saved, to please the teacher or prove you are better than the teacher.

This "sick effort" is fueled by fear. The different flavors in which sick effort comes can be usefully related to unbalanced expressions of the elements: earth, water, fire and air. Space, the fifth element, works a little differently and is not included in this discussion. Here are some notes about how *unbalanced* elements manifest in our approach to our sadhana.

EARTH. You are rigid in your practice, turning it into something mechanical, plodding and mundane. You are so anxious about following procedures in your sadhana that you can't relax. You believe that if you follow the rules, you will get the reward that you want. You become upset if the rules are changed. You are moralistic and critical when other people don't seem to be doing things the "right" way.

WATER. You are needy and sticky in your approach to sadhana. You seek and are dependent on big emotions: outpourings of yearning, prayer, begging, bargaining, weeping, protestations of love and so on. In contrast to real *bhakti*, or surrender through love, this kind of sick effort expresses a fundamental feeling of lack of nourishment and loneliness. You are trying to seduce God into giving you what you want by hyping up your emotions. But these dramatic efforts actually cut you off from receiving the freely-flowing nourishment you crave in your practice and from others.

FIRE. You feel dissatisfaction, frustration, self-doubt and distrust of your capacity to meet and digest what life brings you. You approach spiritual practice with the intention of driving through and burning up these obstacles. You work with the attitude that you will overcome in spite of everything and everyone. You practice long hours with intense focus. You may actually cause your health to deteriorate as you seek to be saved from self-doubt by racking up spiritual "accomplishments." You compulsively seek more accomplishment, more practices, more initiations. You may appear to some to be a consummate yogi, but inside you desperately want approval, recognition and acceptance.

AIR. You are blown around by anxiety, mental overcrowding and a general feeling of fragmentation. You expend a lot of energy moving among a variety of teachers and practices, or being paralyzed by a feeling of being overwhelmed by variety and detail. You complain that you have too much to do. At the same time, sitting quietly without activity terrifies you. You have trouble settling down to a regular pattern of sadhana. You are exhausting yourself by engaging in constant interrupted, irregular, nonproductive activity.

Recognizing these imbalances is the first step. Sometimes simple recognition can bring the capacity to make adjustments in your bhava, or feeling-orientation to sadhana. You can rediscover the sincere desire to relax your tensions and grow.

Because each of these styles of imbalance relates to the expressions of the elements, you can usefully address them through changes in your routines of eating, sleeping and daily conduct. Ayurveda, and other natural life traditions, can help you to recalibrate the expressions of the elements in your body and life.

By adjusting your daily life conduct, healthy expressions of the elements can begin to emerge. These are wisdom virtues such as adaptability; the ability to give and receive proper nourishment; mental, emotional and physical steadiness; clarity, discrimination, both physical and psychic digestive efficiency; and feelings of connectedness.

But if you are experiencing sick effort, it is also important to consult your teachers. Certain kinds of practices can make your imbalances worse, as can the wrong kind of physical activity. Students who attempt to go it alone, learning from hearsay, or only out of books, are at risk of creating more impediments to relaxation, even when intentions are sincere.

Cultivating a sense of humor about oneself and a lighter approach to life in general is also important. When we experience imbalances, we tend to swing between self-congratulation and despair, or we hang out in one of these states. Both over-earnestness and precarious states of false confidence are impediments to relaxing sick effort. Learn to poke loving fun at yourself, and be willing to place all the confidence you can muster in the natural process of unfoldment, aka sadhana.

By doing consistent sadhana, we come to relax and live in harmony with the unimpeded flow of the natural state. We slowly, slowly unwind our fear and rediscover life as an infinitely nuanced, moving palette of expressions. We drop the effort of manufacturing experiences and participate with equanimity in the groundless state of experiencing.

Paradoxically, we do need to work hard to relax. We must apply effort on the path to effortlessness. But it is best to work hard like water.

Water is the foundation of all growth and new life. Water is the fundamental source of nourishment. The balanced water element flows, adapts, shines, dances, plays and meets everything in its path with grace, constancy, sweetness, and both softness and strength. So, try to drop the struggle and apply water-like effort: persistent, smooth, adaptable, dancing and sweet.

DEVOTION

*Devotion is the fruit of all practice because Reality
is made of devotion.*

THIS SHARED LIFE

ONE OF THE meanings of the word "Tantra" is "continuity." A
simple way of understanding continuity is to recognize that we
live in a responsive world. It is not possible to move or change one
thing without the whole of Reality responding in some way.

Most of us have slept in a bed with another person. We know that
if the other person rolls over during the night, we feel the blanket
move. We are also affected.

Our companion might be considerate and try not to move the
blanket too much, but there is no such thing as one side of a blanket moving and the other side remaining totally static. The blanket
moves all at once. This is the way a blanket functions.

Even if we are rigid dualists, we know that our blanket is shared. If
we fall asleep while our companion is reading a book by candlelight,
and later on the candle tips over and sets the blanket on fire, we are
going to jump out of bed! We are not going to remain under a burn-

ing blanket and stupidly proclaim: *I don't care, that is your side of the blanket, not mine!*

We are even going to be helpful and try to put out the fire, or phone the fire department. And after we are sure that everyone is safe and sound, we might insist that our companion not read by candlelight. Maybe we will go out and buy a little lamp just to make sure. In these situations, we take measures to keep ourselves and our loved ones healthy and safe.

But in many other situations, we don't. Maybe a faucet is dripping in our bathroom for months and months, and we just don't get around to fixing it. Or we use toxic chemicals to clean our house. Or we throw old paint down the drain, or if we are American, we buy a big, gas guzzling car.

Many of us don't think about the animals who will suffer and die when those chemicals get into the water system. And we don't wonder where our water is coming from and how many resources it takes to make it drinkable again after we have fouled it. We eat foods laced with pesticides, and we breathe in combustion fumes while first world countries pour billions of dollars into healthcare and the "cancer" research that supports rich scientific institutions. Much of the poverty of our world results from the misuse of land, natural resources and animals.

At its simplest and most elegant, nonduality means everything is shared. We live in a shared world, and even our own bodies are shared bodies. Nothing belongs only to one individual. We are one, continuous body with the capacity to have "many body" experiences.

The reality of your life is that you cannot take a single breath without the cooperation of an entire world.

We can understand this on a gross level, such as in the example of the blanket. We can also talk about the world as a system in which every action eventually affects every part of the system. But this does not get to the heart of the matter.

To most people, it appears that reality is made up of sharply distinct objects. For a long time, modern physics has been fixated on finding the smallest object as if this would uncover the essence of reality.

Our insistence on the independent object as the single defining characteristic of reality stems from *anavamala*. Anavamala is our root sense of separation, or our conviction that we are separate individuals. In Kashmir Shaivism, anavamala is the root form of ignorance, or our root limitation.

Anavamala is a karmic tension. If you have a tension in your neck, you won't be able to turn your head very well. You may not be able to drive a car if the tension gets too bad because your range of vision will be impaired. Human limitation begins with anavamala—our rigid identification with "my self" and "my body."

As long as we are subject to the tension of anavamala, our range of vision, our ability to directly perceive and participate in the more subtle appearings of our world, is also impaired. We do sadhana to relax anavamala.

Mantra practice is often the easiest way to begin to relax anavamala because the gross vibration of the mantra softens our experience of being in a distinctly separate body. When we do relax, we begin to better perceive our shared state.

As we continue in our sadhana, our perceptions of shared life become more direct and immediate. Our senses begin to wake up their subtle capacities, and we can begin to directly perceive the "one taste" or *eka rasa* of everything.

We will eventually come to directly perceive the special intelligence of each of the five elements and their entrance into the manifest world as color and subtle light.

We will experience subtle vibrations and come to understand the inherent wisdom that is at all times being communicated. We may begin to notice the pervasive luminosity of the awake, natural state.

Self-realization does not mean sinking into undifferentiated bliss or transcending human life. Individual experience and the appearings of objects are real experiences of Shiva nature. They are meant to be enjoyed, but they are not the whole story. The aim of all Tantrik sadhana is to experience everything from the perspective of the continuity of consciousness and energy.

Sadhana assists us to de-identify with "my self" and "my body" and begin to re-identify with the shared foundation of the world. When the appearings of shared Reality begin to break through in the course of our lives as practitioners, the dripping of the water from our faucet strikes us very differently. Now, the water is experienced as our own body, as if our own blood were flowing down the drain.

"Our body" has become much larger. We recognize ourselves within and as one with the weave of a single Reality.

In one often told story, Anandamayi Ma once ordered that an newly poured cement sidewalk at an ashram be dug up because it had inadvertently been placed over a young pepper plant. Mataji said she heard the plant calling to her for help.

When we relax anavamala, we receive many kinds of communications from the diverse forms of life that make up our shared life. The world becomes a much richer place for us, and a much less lonely place.

The spectacular beauty of our world is that we can relate as two and as one at the same time. We can hold one and two together and discover the wellsprings of compassion. This is the meaning of shared, and the simple feeling of shared is something we can all work with in our lives, every day.

ADVENTURING IN THE DARK

One of the ways that practitioners begin to relax and enter more fully into sadhana is through dissatisfaction, boredom and disappointment.

You feel that something in your practice isn't working. What is it? You believe you have followed your teacher's instructions to the letter, but nothing seems to be going right, according to your *concept* of "going right," of course.

When people begin a spiritual practice, they generally have some idea of what the fruits should be. They want to find peace, acquire special abilities or become "enlightened" according to their concept of enlightenment.

But any idea you have of the fruits of practice is limited by your current condition.

This is why it is always advised to practice without being attached to a preconceived goal. You should do your sadhana with the bhava of an adventurer or explorer. What will you find? Practice in a state of expectancy, not with expectations.

When you do begin to relax and taste greater spaciousness and equanimity, small I starts to realize that its days are numbered; it is not going to keep getting its fixation fix! So it throws tantrums, hoping to distract you.

You become desperate, so desperate that you will even keep up your practice in spite of your "self." You just don't know what else to do. It seems that your world is falling apart. Everything small I thought, felt, or tried is coming to nothing.

Sadhana is your life raft, but you don't even know where you are headed. You have lost all sense of goal and direction.

This is a good sign. Now is the time to just keep going, even in darkness. Great confidence can be won at this point as the life process takes over and carries you into deeper surrender.

Sadhana is not a step-by-step plan for self-improvement, or for acquiring power, fame and wealth. It is not a miracle drug. Sadhana is a magnifying glass and a mirror. It shows us both our tensions and our inherent capacity for spontaneity, compassion, devotion and freedom of expression.

Sadhana is the greatest adventure you will ever undertake. It is like traveling the deep oceans, the wild forests, the cold, sharp mountains, and outer space.

It is open-ended, limitless, surprising and incomparably creative.

You will encounter yourself, all of yourself. You will be naked, shivering and cold. You will experience every emotion, and eventually you will begin to become aware of and embody the true wisdoms of compassion, grace and unconditional love.

Self-improvement, pleasure, power, fame, miracles and so on are dull, dry dust compared to the fruit of coming into the blazing, aware livingness of Reality.

I AM GURU, HE IS THIEF

This story is often told in my lineage.

A thief used to come and steal from Swami Sivananda's ashram in Rishikesh. During a festival, the ashram was giving *prasad*, (consecrated gifts), in the form of blankets and other necessities to poor people living in the area. The thief came to be given this prasad.

Prasad is food blessed in a ritual invoking a Guru or deity.

Some residents of the ashram came to Swami Sivananda and advised him not to give prasad to the thief. They felt that the thief had already taken many things; why should Swami Sivananda give him more?

Swamiji answered simply: *Thieving is what he does. Giving is what I do.*

Many times in life, we feel that we don't want to be generous unless we get the response, or validation we are seeking.

We don't want to be generous, or loving unless the other person is generous and loving back to us. We don't want to work hard, or do a good job unless we will be praised and tangibly rewarded.

Sometimes we say we are being "nice" or "compassionate," but really we are just avoiding responsibility for our life, using the other person as an excuse.

On the other hand, people often say: *I can't do what I want to do because so-and-so won't like it.* We do some things to win recognition and praise, and we don't do other things in order to avoid rejection and criticism.

Our fundamental relationship to the world is manipulative. We are always bargaining and cutting deals.

We suffer because we demand that other people play by the rules of our karmic vision. Then we are disappointed when they fail to do this. For instance, we have an idea of how "true love" should display itself, and we expect other people to enact this drama exactly as we imagine it should be.

Why can't she be more like I want her to be? What's wrong with that person! Why doesn't she feel the way I do?

In fact, most of the conversations people have about their intimate relationships consist of complaining about how other people feel and act.

In order to begin to release this form of karmic tension, it is important to understand two things.

First, every person has a unique dimension – their own unique configuration. No matter how you feel about it, or how good or bad that uniqueness looks to you, every being is doing Shiva nature perfectly. The number one wisdom virtue we want to express in our relationships is to respect each person's unique dimension.

Respecting each others' unique dimensions doesn't mean we have to put up with any kind of behavior. We can choose to be with, or not be with people. It does mean *actually respecting* their right to express Shiva nature in any way, even if we don't like it. There is nothing fundamentally wrong with anyone.

Second, complaining and criticizing are modes of relating.

Divine impulse, divine wisdom, naturally impels us to connect. Even when we are complaining about others, we are still trying to connect. However, karmic tension creates limitation on our ability to discover a more natural continuity with life. For instance, I may be chronically disappointed in some other person, and that person is in my thoughts continuously. I am actually connecting, although in a way that will not bring me the intimacy for which I long.

When we begin to relax our karmic vision and discover our natural continuity with the whole, the diversity of life is no longer so threatening to us. We no longer are trying to manipulate others into assuaging our tensions. We can just be ourselves and, at the same time, truly respect the unique dimensions of others.

TANTRA, DEVOTION, INQUIRY

Devotion and humble service are like kneading a lump of heavy, cold dough until it becomes soft, pliable and warm.

Inquiry, or asking questions and freely using your mind and your senses to explore and discover your real condition, is like the yeast that allows the softened dough to rise above dogma and fixation.

Guru is the heat that cooks the bread.

We all know that without kneading and yeast, no amount of heat will make a loaf of bread cook properly. A lump will remain a lump. So, when we are not softened by a feeling of devotion and relieved of our dogma by a spirit of free inquiry, we cannot fully receive transmission from Guru, or from Reality at large. Our senses are too gross to receive more subtle communications.

Through transmission, the Guru provides shocks of Self-recognition and continually challenges us to let go of our limitations and expand. This chemistry of cooking between student and teacher is the mechanism that our own enlightened Self has given to us. We become more aware of our grossness, and our senses become more subtle just by being around Guru and doing our sadhana with that person's guidance.

Guru and disciple is one natural technology, a perfectly natural "recipe." But even in the company of Guru, we still must learn through our own senses, the mind being also a sense. No teacher can make us become more aware if we are not doing some "kneading and rising." Gurus lead us to our Self, but they cannot save us.

As our senses become less clogged, we receive more and more understanding directly from our teacher, and from the world at large. Eventually, perhaps after many lifetimes, we are in no need of one teacher because our senses are more fully alive. We discover that all knowledge is knowledge of our own Self, given by Self to Self in the magnificent play of life.

JO HO JAYE

Anandamayi Ma often repeated the phrase *jo ho jaye*. Live by these three words and you will discover all View, all method and all fruit.

Jo ho jaye is usually translated as " Whatever happens happens," or " Wait for whatever happens."

Jo ho jaye is not a statement of fatalism or nihilism: *It is an instruction for surrendering and taking refuge in life.*

Life is happening. Only tension causes us to take up a particular stance toward this ongoingness, for instance, that I like it or I don't like it, or that it is good or bad, beautiful or ugly.

Try to relax your compulsion to accept, reject, categorize, fix, predict and manipulate everything. Use your practice to develop more sensitivity to what actually is unfolding and to respond and adapt to that. Learn to follow life's lead. This is real surrender.

Small I has lots of limited desires. It aggressively pursues the objects of those limited desires. Like a race horse with blinders on, small I often misses out on the free flowing, open creativity of life.

Small I operates under the illusion that it chooses and decides via its own individual will and can therefore get what it desires. As long as we continue choosing, deciding, planning, and projecting from the point of View of small I, we reinforce our tensions.

Even happiness derived from these activities of small I is limited by fear of losing what we believe we have gained. When we relax and follow the promptings of cosmic wisdom, we move more quickly in the direction of Self-realization.

After doing sadhana for a time, when the possibility of deeper relaxation comes into View, people often feel fear recognizing that they will have to surrender to life. They will have to stop asking incessantly: *What should I do? How should I live?* They will be called upon to relinquish their problem-solving approach and let the totality of life direct all of their activities.

Our teachers can give us a glimpse of a life guided by the promptings of wisdom inherent in all circumstances. We can be inspired by stories of those who have gone before us. But the fact is that we cannot develop full confidence in Life, in the world Self, until we consciously begin to open our senses and allow ourselves to be guided. For most of us, this happens little-by-little, step-by-step.

Remembering jo ho jaye can support us in this process.

DETOURS

There are many ways of getting stuck, or waylaid on the path to waking up, but freedom is always victorious. The only question is: When?

KNOWLEDGE IS BONDAGE

ATTACHMENT TO CONCEPTUALIZING, categorizing, capturing and displaying knowledge undermines spiritual practice. I have met people who are so unwilling to be seen as beginners, or to make a mistake, or to take the smallest leap into the unknown, they cannot even begin a spiritual practice. They are completely paralyzed by attachment to knowing.

Others demand to know exactly what they will get from sadhana before they start. Or, they come to a teacher having already decided what it is they want to know. They want to acquire certain practices or knowledge as if the teacher and the teachings were a supermarket from which to pick and choose. This happens among students of even the most accomplished teachers.

A more common phenomenon is that students feel unable to follow what are called "pointing out" instructions. These are key instructions for aspects of sadhana that can never be technically precise. Upon being given a transmission of pointing out instructions, the student must intuit what needs to be done.

The teacher uses certain phrases that suggest a method, or a destination, but the student has to feel her way. People who are anxious about knowing precisely what to do, or who are over reliant on intellect, often have trouble following pointing out instructions.

In general, many people find themselves in a state of resistance to the simple, relaxed, open-ended exploration of which authentic sadhana consists. We have an idea of where it should all lead, and we are attached to that idea.

Being in control of knowing and knowledge is the way that people manage their overwhelming fear of the boundless flow of reality. We stake out our tiny little claim in the vast universe. Then we cling to our limited understanding.

Attachment to knowing more, knowing specific techniques, spiritual achievements, and winning approval for what we know will *never* lead to realization. These pleasures must be surrendered.

It is painful to stop feeding these sweets to yourself. But an even deeper surrender is required.

At some point, even the conceptual understandings given to you by your tradition to help you on your way must be given up. You will just be here, feeling everything and finding out for yourself.

EMBODIED UNDERSTANDING VS. BORROWED KNOWLEDGE

Embodied understanding means that the fruit of your practice shows up in every area of your life: waking, sleeping and dreaming. You feel, look, behave, eat and play according to the fruit of your practice.

Embodied understanding emerges over time when you have had good View teachings and consistently do practices that involve your energy, your senses, and your mind. It comes out of your entire being, not just your mouth.

Students, and even teachers, often trade in borrowed knowledge. Borrowed knowledge is conceptual. You've read it in a book, or you've heard it "around," or from someone else. You have not actually practiced to realize this understanding. You have not integrated this knowledge into your life, but you profess it to others as if it *were* your own embodied knowledge.

Borrowed knowledge can be delivered in the form of helpful advice to fellow practitioners; theories, opinions, pronouncements or musings; or by taking up the mantle of the teacher or Guru.

Borrowed knowledge often hops a ride when someone has practiced something—asana, a mantra or meditation—and professes to have realized much beyond what has actually been embodied. This is much more likely to happen when a person has not had thorough, or any instruction. The tendency is to over-interpret some minor result.

Borrowed knowledge always serves an identity construct. We wave the banner of our borrowed knowledge to assuage our fears and insecurities and as a method of self-pleasuring. Sometimes people build entire spiritual careers on largely borrowed knowledge. Borrowed knowledge is a great hindrance to real spiritual growth.

Embodied knowledge does not depend on books, theories, belief, faith, trust or opinions. We can read about our traditions and receive View teachings that correctly orient us to our practice. But in the end, only by doing consistent sadhana do we come to embody a fuller Reality.

If I want to raise and lower my arm, reading a book about how the arm works will not help me. Neither will talking or theorizing about arms. I just have to try it.

I could gather every kind of scientist and philosopher in a room and try to arrive at a complete description of how to raise and lower my arm, but they will not be able to produce one. Something will always be left out. More importantly, the description itself can never guarantee that I will actually succeed in performing the act of raising and lowering my arm.

Embodied knowledge can never be completely captured in a description. It can only be arrived at by practice and transmitted by someone who has realized that knowledge.

My experience in the U.S. is that people, in a kind of innocent way, often cannot tell the difference between embodied understanding and borrowed knowledge. People are firmly entrenched in the concept that intellectual understanding *is* understanding. This concept itself becomes embodied knowledge and literally blocks students from being able to let go and learn in a real way.

People have forgotten how to use their senses, body and more subtle energy to learn. Minds are reduced to thinking machines. The capacity to use the mind properly as the sense organ of curiosity is atrophied.

The practices of direct realization traditions are powerful. Done over a long period of time, they will entirely remake you. When we rely on borrowed knowledge, we are basically admitting that we don't understand the practices, or respect them. We are also robbing ourselves of the opportunity to actually find out.

Apprenticing yourself, day-by-day, to the process of unfoldment, you can come to live a life of total relaxation, creativity, spontaneity, compassion and wonder. Your birthright is to embody all of the wisdom virtues of Shiva nature. Compared to this, borrowed knowledge is a dry twig blowing in the wind.

In order to grow, you must look deeply into what the Daoist tradition calls your "treasury of worms." You have to face up to your own fears and tensions in order to relax them. Borrowed knowledge prevents this process from unfolding naturally.

Letting go of all the ways in which you build fortresses out of borrowed knowledge means being willing to make mistakes, lumber around, embrace your confusion and, most of all, encounter the openness of "I don't know."

Practitioners need to learn how to *reach out* to Reality with their entire beings. They must learn, and in some cases relearn, how to actually find out.

Think of how a baby learns to walk. This is how you need to do your practice. Step-by-step, feeling your way, getting up when you fall, crying when you need to cry, and continuing on with both determination and delight.

Letting go, without the support of our concepts, beliefs and convictions, can feel scarily insecure. Openness scares us, at the same time that we long for it.

But the longing we feel is really our best friend. It is the voice of Guru cutting through our limitations. Our longing for "something" is precisely our embodied understanding. And it's calling out for us to stop talking so much, practice more and relax into not knowing so embodied understanding can arise.

SPIRITUAL TALK

Contrary to popular opinion, talk is not cheap. *Vak* means speech, word, language and sound. Vak is the primordial form of the Goddess, of Shakti. When we speak excessively and unnecessarily, we lose Shakti and become depleted.

While talk is not cheap, spiritual talk is the most expensive of all. Spiritual talk falls into two main categories: talking about our spiritual experiences and offering opinions about spiritual practice and View.

When we share a spiritual experience with all and sundry, we dissipate the Shakti we should be using to make the View of that experience our new home base.

Spiritual experiences are not the end of practice, they are work orders.

Spiritual experience is a transmission and a call to do the work to stabilize and embody a new level of understanding. In order to do this, we need to contain and concentrate our energy.

Nine times out of ten, when people talk about their spiritual experiences, they are bragging and soliciting the admiration of others. This bragging can sound terribly humble and fool everyone. You can even fool yourself. But at the end of the day (the end of your life), you will be just as prideful, fear-driven and anxiety-ridden as ever. And even if there was some authenticity in the experiences you blabbed about over and over again, the wisdom will have been lost.

This does not mean that spiritual experiences should never be mentioned by anyone. Teachers talk about their own experiences, or those of others, to assist students in various ways. But you'll notice that most teachers are very sparing in this regard. More often, teachers talk about spiritual experiences in private, one-on-one with students they believe will be helped by this at a particular stage of development.

In fact, you *should* relate your experiences to your teacher. A good teacher will be able to tell you something about the significance of the phenomena that arise as a result of sadhana. A teacher can also tell you about the phenomena that arise as a result of fantasy! Telling our experiences to a qualified teacher is an important part of developing discrimination and receiving proper guidance.

By far the most expensive form of spiritual talk is spiritual opinionism.

In most spiritual communities, and certainly in on-line spiritual communities, many opinions about spiritual practice and View are offered freely and frequently. Generally, those offering spiritual opinions do so with great confidence, smoothness and verve.

We live in a culture that values knowing and information. We are extremely well-trained in conceptual thinking and giving ready answers. In fact, we are trained in school and by our parents to sound like we are sure of ourselves even when we are not.

All of this cultural training is at odds with the skills we need to enter into an authentic spiritual practice: a high tolerance for uncertainty, an attitude of soft openness to life and a willingness to allow life to unfold without imposing too many conceptual grids upon it.

In order to grow, we must learn to listen deeply and follow what we hear.

Quiet, deep listening is key. It is much better for you to listen and follow than it is to talk and lead.

Whether you are racing around, gathering information from multiple sources, or standing on the corner handing it out, you are not listening. While you are exercising your cultural skills of knowing, informing, and explicating; while you are considering the ten different bits of advice you got today, the Goddess Paravak, the supreme speech of cosmic wisdom is being outshouted.

Many people do not have a teacher who is readily accessible. You may only see your teacher now and then. Or your teacher may be extremely busy. In these cases, you should ask your teacher if there is someone working under her to whom you can go for more regular guidance. Your teacher might also suggest reading material. It is always better to seek advice from your teacher than to try to find out on your own from the Internet, random books or other people.

KARMIC ENTANGLEMENT

When we are doing Tantrik, or any kind of spiritual practice, or just living our lives, we want to move toward a condition of less tension, attachment and emotional fixation. These are the symptoms and textures of karma.

Karma means limited activity. Karma is consciousness and energy repeating a pattern of limitation in time. What creates limited activity is limited View.

For instance, a person has the View that she is second best and is always in danger of being passed over. This View engenders a habit pattern of vigilance and competitiveness. She is always trying to overcome her inner feeling of second best by proving externally that she is better than everyone. This person gets stuck in this pattern until she learns more about her real nature.

The more someone with this karmic patterning keeps fighting and struggling to prove herself, the deeper and wider the entanglement will become. She will create new situations with other people that express her tension. These situations will need to be resolved.

The time and energy it takes to resolve karmic entanglements is time and energy taken away from your practice.

Most people cannot go through life without creating at least some further entanglement. This is the human condition. Most of us are not going to be able to resolve all of our karma in one lifetime.

But those of us on a conscious path of waking up should try to minimize the degree to which we create more tension within ourselves and project that onto people and situations. If you reduce your level of entanglement, you will experience more clarity and energy in your practice and more freedom of expression in this life. You will also have the freedom to move toward a more expansive form of existence as you are passing through the bardos of death.

In all of our karmic fixations, there is always an element of pleasure. Pleasure is actually the root of attachment. We experience pleasure even as we are suffering. This is obvious when we are talking about a karmic pattern such as food, drug or alcohol addiction. But it's also true about emotions we chronically generate such as frustration, anger and jealousy.

All karmic patterning, no matter how limited, is an attempt to resolve the root ignorance: our feeling of separation from others, and ultimately, from our own enlightened nature. We are trying to connect no matter how misguided our efforts may be.

The pleasure at the heart of fixation is some momentary experience of intimacy, satisfaction or fulfillment. If we are violent toward others, we are still trying to connect. However connecting with a fist does not get the result we most deeply want. When we subsequently go to jail, this creates a situation in which we are made even more aware of the pain of separation.

I call this "bad stop." We should have stopped going in the direction of entanglement and exhaustion long ago, but we ignored all the warning signs. Now we are forcibly stopped. Everything that happens is grace. Bad stop is fierce grace.

We all go through this exact same process in ten thousand different ways. If we go the route of acting out our limited View, we end up at some point feeling our separation more. This continues until we feel our loneliness and longing so directly, that we finally get how necessary it is to make more successful efforts to connect. Once we discover what we really want, we can begin to direct our efforts toward the only lasting fulfillment: the discovery of our real nature and our intimacy with everything.

So, the first step is to recognize your karmic habit patterns and to try to feel and listen for the loneliness and longing they express. Try to feel deeply the divine longing at the heart of even your most limited habits of body, energy and mind. When you connect with your longing in this way, you will also discover more compassion for yourself.

Having felt it, you then have to take 100 percent responsibility for this longing. It's not someone else's job to fulfill your needs. And it won't work even if you demand that from another person. We can support each other and accompany each other and comfort each other, but in the end, no one can walk the path to fulfillment for you.

Determine within yourself, that you will do your best not to drag yourself or others deeper into entanglement. Use your practice day-by-day to relax, take nourishment and renew. Let the longing grow in you and find its proper object: to know your Self.

Organize your life so that everything you do, or do not do, has the goal of protecting your practice. Don't cheat, lie, steal or get involved in situations that will tie up your energy in guilt, regret, argument or litigation.

This advice is not about right or wrong, good or bad, sinful or pure. You have to functionally manage your energy and your level of entanglement in this way in order to protect your practice and experience greater peace and freedom in your life.

UPSET WITH GURU? LOOK IN THE MIRROR!

Students miss opportunities to realize by treating what arises in relationship with their teachers in an ordinary way. This most often manifests when students get upset with a teacher's behavior or attitudes and then expend a lot of energy analyzing the teacher.

The relationship with Guru is for only one thing: Self-realization. What you should be doing is examining yourself in the mirror of the teacher.

The *melong* is a metal disk, polished to a mirror finish. Melong are living symbols of the natural process of teacher and student working together.

The teacher serves as a mirror into which the student can look and see his true image reflected. By fearlessly gazing into the melong, over time, students can clarify and expand their View and release themselves from limitation and fixation.

If you are a student who has found a real teacher, you should try to see everything that transpires between you as phenomena arising for your benefit in the mirror of the open state of teacher.

If the teacher does something that angers, humiliates or annoys you, spending a lot of time analyzing the teacher's personality or behavior will cause you to miss an opportunity to relax and grow. You are only delaying your Self-realization if you focus on "what the teacher did to me," or how you think the teacher should have spoken to you, or what the teacher, in your opinion, should have done differently.

The teacher is the melong, the mirror. The focus of your inquiry should always be what you see in the mirror and your own reactivity.

For instance, I told a student a story about myself and my diksha Guru. For some months, when I would come and go, he would never say hello, or goodbye. Even if I traveled long distances to receive teachings, he did not take any special notice of my arrival, or bother to mark my leaving.

How rude! my student immediately commented.

Not so. My teacher was reflecting attachments with which I needed to work. Only by causing me the pain of feeling those attachments more acutely, could I notice them enough to work directly to relax them. He was also giving me a living View teaching: We live in total continuity: there is no coming and no going.

My teacher was inviting me to greater realization. If I had reacted in an ordinary way, as did my student, I would have lost the opportunity. My real job was to notice my own suffering and to work with that using the tools of sadhana.

Of course, my teacher was deliberately provoking my reactivity. This is the norm in Tantrik lineages. Those who gravitate toward this way of working with the teacher generally *want* to be provoked so that they can see their own tensions clearly and relax them more quickly. For this reason, Tantra is a fierce path.

But there were lots of things my teacher did that provoked me, and others, that were *not* deliberate. Most teachers are not highly, or fully realized. They have their own tensions and blind spots.

Students, especially in the U.S., make the mistake of trying to separate out the "realized" from the "not realized" aspects of their teachers. Again, this is putting the emphasis on the wrong party. The emphasis should always be on *your reactivity*, not on your teacher's.

You are there to work with yourself in the crucible of the student-teacher relationship. Understand that everything that happens is part of the alchemy of this relationship whose only purpose is to help *you* to wake up. This includes all aspects of the teacher's personality: love it, or hate it.

Even the "bad" things a good teacher does, can be useful for a good student who is working with her reactivity. This does not mean everyone should remain with any teacher no matter what the circumstance. Of course you want to develop enough clarity so that you can avoid, or learn from and then leave, teachers who are not yet embodying the fruits of practice.

It does mean that if you *are* working with a teacher, you will get the best result for you if you treat the entire circumstance as the teaching.

STICKINESS ON THE SPIRITUAL PATH

Someone once said to me: *I don't know how you've done it, but somehow you've managed not to get stuck in all the ways spiritual aspirants usually get stuck.*

This is no mystery. I've had teachers prying me loose at every sticky turn.

Stickiness is attachment to people, relationships, experiences and concepts, especially self-concept. It all adds up to one big sticky gumball. All attachment is an attempt by small self to keep itself stuck together in a more or less static form.

I came into this world with attachments and developed new ones along the way. Many of our attachments are obvious. Some are very subtle. Treading the spiritual path can be like spending years trapped in a fun house. If you are practicing well, all of the attachments you never knew you had will pop out, do a scary dance and laugh a scary laugh.

A special category of stickiness is attachment to spiritual concepts, projections and experiences.

How about that special spiritual dream you had three months ago that you are still talking about? Or the special spiritual voice you talk in to let everyone know you are spiritual? Or the fizzy sensation you once had that you worked up into a "kundalini" experience. And now you refer to it as "my samadhi?"

These are gross forms of spiritual fixation. These are obvious ways that small I condenses around spiritual stuff. Same old smallness, just glossier stories. This sort of indulgence will not free you.

But all spiritual practitioners, even sincere ones, can easily get stuck. We get stuck because we are not taught proper View. We get stuck because we don't have a large enough perspective on Reality to guide us past our fixations. We absolutely need View, and imparting

View to a student is the most important job of any teacher.

The Sanskrit word for View is "*darshan*." Darshan has many meanings. You might hear people talking about "getting darshan" from a teacher. This means seeing a teacher and receiving a transmission of the essence state. This transmission expands your View.

View teachings often come in the form of oral or written transmissions of the nature of Reality and how to realize that.

For instance, teachings about the nature of Reality and the stages of spiritual unfoldment are View teachings. So is the teaching that whenever you hold onto a certain stage of development or experience, you are in danger of organizing it into another self-concept and of ceasing to grow.

View teachings guide you through times when you are in danger of falling into mistaken ideas and practices due to your limited attachments and ignorance of Nature. Ignorance of Nature is non-realization. Realization is living the View, or embodying an understanding of how things are.

People are naturally drawn to realizing their own nature. Your desire to wake up is the Shakti that drives the life process of Shiva nature.. You learn to detach from what is sticking you to limitation, and you attach to that which will help you to wake up.

Your sticky attachments are limited expressions of the same more generalized, expansive capacity to attach to that which guides you to Self-realization. See how the world works? Gorgeous!

Attaching to our Guru, ishta devata and spiritual community is the leap that we make when we are moving to a less contracted, self-limiting state of attachment. The world, in its infinite grace, gives us these manifest guides to attach to so that we can cultivate our own awakeness, which is ultimately groundless.

GUILT AND REGRET

Many people suffer from a tension they call "guilt."

Guilt is a tricky little small I survival pattern. Guilt uses the mask of responsibility to avoid responsibility and maintain destructive habit patterns.

If we act or don't act and then claim to feel guilty about it, what is really going on?

Guilt is one hundred percent "me" focused.

Guilt draws attention away from the reality of my actions and toward small self's feeling of guilt. By feeling really guilty, I try to fool everyone into thinking I am taking responsibility, but I am actually running away from responsibility and sucking energy out of others.

Usually, guilt demands sympathy from those very others who have been most affected by my action or inaction. Guilt is "me" focused instead of Real Situation focused. Guilt is a technique for evading responsible action.

If we injure an animal with our car, we try to do something to alleviate the animal's suffering. We don't stand idly at the curb moaning about how guilty we feel about the plight of animals. We don't demand that others attend to our guilt while leaving the actual animal to suffer alone. Or maybe we do.

Guilt always tries to perpetuate itself. Have you ever tried to talk a person out of feeling guilty? Guilt just uses this attention to fuel itself. No matter how sensible and Reality-based you are with a guilty person, they can always return to the status quo by claiming *I feel so guilty!*

In this way, cultivating guilt helps to keep the guilty person primed and ready to return to the same irresponsible behaviors.

How does this work?

Guilt is a pay out. You do something destructive to yourself and others. Then you pay for your behavior with the "punishment" of feeling guilty. After this, you are free to return to the same pattern. Or likely you are in the pattern and feeling guilty all at the same time. You pay as you go.

Guilty people also apologize without any real intention of changing their situation. Even worse is when they ask for forgiveness. Instead of quietly and efficiently rectifying their behavior, they ask someone else to perform the work of a priest.

For people who are stuck with guilt, this pattern usually happens over and over again. It's really exhausting. The guilty should get angry at guilt and its ploys. Guilt is like a bad houseguest who eats your food and leaves you with an enormous utility bill.

The truth is, none of us needs to be forgiven for our ignorance. Having an experience of limitation is just a natural aspect of the life process. But you might want to take some steps to try to wake up.

Waking up is being responsible to your real situation. You have the opportunity to practice and discover more of your human situation and its potentials, and you seize this opportunity.

A friend told me he felt guilty about something. Then he said, *I suppose Tantrikas don't feel guilty.*

True. But we do feel healthy regret. When we regret our actions, we are saying that we see their consequences, and we intend to do our best to relax the tensions that caused us to act in a certain ignorant way.

Regret acknowledges that we cannot change what has already happened, but we can have an impact on what is going to happen. This is responsibility without whining or narcissism.

Regret acknowledges the harm we have caused to ourselves and others, but it doesn't wring pity out of people.

No matter how destructive a pattern has been, we can always make a decision to use our practice and begin to relax those tensions. We can do better the next time. Sometimes we take vows to help us with this. Sometimes we are able, because of the grace inherent in the totality of a situation, to develop more clarity and change our patterning in that moment.

For people who habitually express their suffering in the form of guilt, to self-recognize what guilt actually is can be an experience like taking a big breath of fresh, cold mountain air.

Relaxing the grip of guilt to let in honest regret also lets in self-compassion and compassion for others. We are no longer locked up in our cage of guilt, continually reinforcing our root sense of separation. We can rejoin the human family, and even appreciate that clever trickster guilt as we say goodbye.

LIFE SUCKS

If you have ever gone swimming in a fast-moving river, you know that you have to be a good observer of state of the river in order to know how to move in keeping with the shifting waters. You have to observe the many currents and rocks and other beings. You need good judgment and timing in order to stay afloat and on course.

This is exactly parallel to our human lives.

Let's say we are doing a good job of balancing on a rock in the middle of the river of life. We are congratulating ourselves because we have managed not to be swept away. Our entire focus is on that rock.

This is how many of us live. We try to keep everything static and safe-feeling while life roars around us.

However, because our focus is so narrow and fixed, we do not see the crocodile coming. Standing so still in the middle of the river, we are perfectly placed to become a meal for the crocodile. All of a sudden—we are dinner!

How did that happen, you wonder from inside the croc's belly! I had everything together, perfectly balanced, and now Life Sucks!

The answer is bad timing brought on by ignorance, aka: narrow View.

In order to act more fluidly and with better timing, we have to encompass a wider View. This is what spiritual practice is for—enlarging our View so that we can embody more spaciousness and presence and avoid being tumbled about by karma, good, or bad.

When we embody a larger View, our senses open up and become more subtle. Our thinking has more clarity. We experience less confusion because some of our karmic entanglement has cleared. We are no longer driven by a sense of anxious urgency, or held in place by lethargy. We are free to move and adapt more skillfully.

Of course, most people on the planet are not Self-realized. So we all have more or less bad timing. This is the human condition.

What can we do?

First, when you hit a hard patch in life, pull yourself out of the misapprehension that you have been victimized, or that life is unfair. Life is uneven, and everything is fine.

On another level, everything that happens "to" you is a response, at least in part, to your activity, and it is a compassionate response. We are always being communicated to in every circumstance in a way that has the possibility to help us to wake up.

On even another level, there is only the world Self, so there is no one to victimize you. Everything that happens is Shiva nature.

You are not being punished for bad timing. You are human, and human life has its ups and downs. Bad timing is unavoidable. It is not a sin. It is a natural part of the life process.

Don't spend too much time trying to figure out how you got yourself into a mess. It's good to reflect on missed signals and the moments in which you ignored your own wisdom. But having done so, move on. Turn your attention to the present. Adapt to your new circumstance and work as skillfully with these as you can.

The river is flowing. A new situation arises in every moment. Being attached to explaining the past is just like clinging to a rock in the river. Eventually, every rock will become sand. So why not let go now and learn to swim?

No matter what happens, you are responsible for how you react to circumstance. For instance, if ten people are in a room with another person who is just learning to play the trombone, there will be ten different reactions.

One person will be intellectually interested in the process of learning an instrument. Another person will feel sympathetic. Yet another person will cringe with humiliation every time the new trombonist makes a mistake. Someone will giggle. Yet another person will feel angry at being stuck in a room with such a noise, and so on.

Think of people who have been through very painful experiences such as incarceration, torture, rape, war and serious illness. Some people make use of these experiences to grow. Others cannot digest their circumstance and become traumatized by anger and fear. Still others, although very few, have done enough spiritual practice that they remain relaxing in their own nature no matter what is happening.

The message here is that your reaction to your life circumstances is *your* reaction, shaped by *your* karma. No one is causing you to react in any particular way.

Although we are responsible for our lives, we do have help. We can slowly improve our timing by enlarging our View. But more immediately, we can consult our teachers, a good astrologer or use a form of divination to help us to better surf the currents of the present.

Our aim in consulting a Guru, astrologer or diviner should be to discern the potentials in the present so that we can take responsibility for our life and use better timing to help create a smoother future. It should *not* be to figure out how we can be saved by predictions of future good fortune. This is unreal, and it is not responsible.

So, when hard times come around, try to relate to that in a simple, practical way. No drama. Just get on with what you need to do in order to take care of the basics of existence.

Although it may seem counter-intuitive to some, when life is difficult, when you seem to have lost everything, that is the best time to offer service to your teacher, community and anyone else who needs it. No matter what your circumstance, you can always be of service, even if it is just by offering a loving gesture to your fellow inmates!

Service helps us to reconnect with our real refuge in the divine Self and rediscover natural nourishment and devotion. It shows us that we have never really lost anything. We are always perfect and complete.

STAR TREK VS. THE KALI YUGA

I grew up watching Star Trek with my mom. Somehow, rationalism, technology and the scientific View have failed to deliver that shiny, clean world of unlimited exploration in which human beings get to lecture less evolved races on other planets about their bad behavior.

Instead, the individualistic greed of our human cultures has injured, not only the space program, but our air, water, land and the lives of millions upon millions of people and animals.

Welcome to the *Kali Yuga*. The Kali Yuga is the final, and darkest, cycle of four epochs that make up the entire wheel of samsaric, linear time. "Darkness" means ignorance. Ignorance is ignorance of one thing only: your real nature.

Beginning with the *Satya Yuga*, the age when people are closest to Self-realization, and therefore have the fewest karmic entanglements with which to contend, human beings descend into greater and greater ignorance with each epoch.

People of each of the yugas benefit most from methods that best address their particular capacities. As the story goes, the appropriate sadhana for most people of the Kali Yuga is mantra japa and kirtan. In the Satya Yuga, more people are capable of engaging in subtle meditation.

Whether or not you have a concrete experience of the yugas, the progression of the four epochs expresses the understanding that Reality has the capacity to beget ignorance and that the deepest ignorance still contains the capacity for realization. Hence, at the end of the final epoch, the Kali Yuga, the cycle begins again with a renewal of the Satya Yuga.

You can see this principle at work today. The extreme violence perpetrated against the nation of Tibet and its people has resulted in

Tibetan Buddhism spreading all over the world. Before the invasion of Tibet, not a single lama was teaching outside of that small, inaccessible country. Now many more people have the opportunity to receive and practice authentic wisdom teachings.

This is, of course, a complex situation. People inside Tibet and those living in the diaspora are still suffering greatly, as are Chinese people, both those who have perpetrated violence and ordinary people. The denial of freedom on an ordinary level is the gross expression of the experience of separation.

The root ignorance, or anavamala, is our conviction that Reality is constituted of distinct entities or objects. Everyone suffers from the embodied View that we are separate beings. This conviction characterizes science, much of philosophy, psychology and contemporary social life.

Physicists search for the basic "particle" of life. Doctors search for the causes of disease in individual genes. We wantonly kill other living beings and destroy our planet because we are cut off from empathy and compassion. It is difficult for most people to think beyond the question of "How does this affect me?"

Modern cultures are driven by the View that we can use mechanistic, scientific means to compensate for the losses in our environment and the toxins eating away at our blood, brains and organs. As we kill off our bodies, piece by piece, we fantasize about being saved by shiny new parts, impervious to death.

Our scientists try to fix, for billions of dollars, what the simple recognition of interdependence and a little everyday compassionate sharing could set right for free.

Luckily for us, in the Kali Yuga, a small, steady, sincere effort to Self-realize goes a long way. This is grace at work in our age.

Look around you. You can easily see that having discovered teachings is a marvelous opportunity. Take full advantage of this circumstance, but don't cultivate any heroic, or superior "spiritual" attitudes. We in the West have done that for a long time. Even spiritual lineages have cultivated competitiveness. The time when such attitudes can be indulged in without recognizing the cruelty they perpetuate has come to an end.

In an age of ignorance, it is best to cultivate gratitude rather than feelings of superiority. It is better to share the fruits of your practice by living alongside those who are mired in ignorance, than to build walls—real walls or attitudinal walls. It is walls that got us here.

There is nothing to struggle against. The world takes care of itself. But we *are* this world, and we have our parts to play. Cultivating your practice so that you are able to express sincere kindness, empathy and compassion is the way to go. If you are able to do this, give thanks. Give great thanks.

DETOURS

One day, I got a speeding ticket. It just so happened that I was engaged in pushing ahead with plans that were not in sync with wisdom. I was being willful rather than responsive to life.

I remarked to someone that getting a speeding ticket and being told by Guru to SLOW DOWN are exactly the same: a meaningful communication from Reality. This person replied that perhaps I was just driving too fast. This is the kind of View that causes people to miss important communications from wisdom over and over again.

There is only continuity. Absolutely everything that arises is a response of Self to Self. Every accomplished practitioner arrives at this insight sooner or later.

If you look, listen, taste, touch, smell and reflect fully, you get to join the total conversation. If your senses and mind are limited, you miss aspects of the conversation entirely, or respond inappropriately.

Wisdom, aka Reality, is always trying to communicate with us. The purpose of the communication is to get us to become more aware and Self-recognize.

If we don't listen to Wisdom, we get another chance, and another and another. Each opportunity grows more insistent like progressively harder knocks on the head. If we still don't listen, then whatever we were clinging to is usually ripped away. This is grace, even though it is painful.

On the other hand, sometimes our resistance is so high, Wisdom responds by offering us a "detour." A detour is when we temporarily get what small I wants.

The detour might be something that brings satisfaction and completes a difficult karma. For instance, perhaps a particular person has the karma of never having fallen in love. To some other person, this might be unimportant, but to this person, the desire to fall in love is dominant. Receiving that experience and feeling satisfied might allow the person to relax and move on.

Another person might have the karma of overeating. This person gets lots of potential opportunities to make a decision to adjust their diet, but they are not ready for that. And so the detour becomes going to the nth degree eating everything and becoming very sick. Eventually, the desire to overeat will be overpowered by the desire to live.

A detour might bring us resolution through fulfillment, or it might temporarily satisfy and then bring us to the point of becoming sick, poor, horribly lonely or subject to some other kind of crisis.

Anandamayi Ma called this taking the long way around. The shorter way is to use your freedom and begin to form new habits *now* that will take you in the direction of natural relaxation and realization. Eventually everyone must face their karmic fixations and choose to relax them. It's just a matter of how long it will take and how much pain you will experience along the way.

A core teaching states that Wisdom never gives us more than we can handle. If an opportunity to relax your tensions arises, you can be sure that if you say *yes*, you will succeed. But you can also say no for a while and extend your suffering. You may think you are choosing greater comfort, but that comfort is exceedingly temporary. It is just padding for your prison cell. At some point you *will* have to come out and play in the openness of life.

We have the experience of being able to choose to remain in ignorance and limitation only up until a certain point. When we reach that point, we have Self-recognized to the degree that we understand Self-realization is nothing other than the inevitable life process. We then become "non-returners." While we will still resist out of habit, we know that resistance is futile.

COMMUNITIES

A spiritual community is a gateway to realizing your continuity with all beings. Through your spiritual community, you realize Maha or Great Community.

COMMUNITY IS SADHANA

TANTRA IS A householder tradition. This means we are living full lives with work, friends, families and even children. We live in villages, towns and cities. We are not generally sitting on mountaintops, or hanging around in caves with only birds, snakes and mosquitos as companions.

We look for the fruit of our practice, in part, in how we show up in our everyday relationships. Our relationships are mirrors that reflect our condition. However, our friends and family may not be engaged in the same spiritual tradition, or any practice at all. For this reason, it is extremely useful to have a *sangha*, or *kula*.

Sangha means the group of people associated with the same teacher, or tradition. Sangha includes those following the practice closely as well as those who might just come for satsang, or some other occasional teachings.

Kula is a specifically Tantrik term meaning "family." In ancient days, it meant those who had received diksha and who lived with their Guru. Today, kula can mean the initiated students of a teacher, or those with a deep commitment to the teachings and to doing sadhana.

Spiritual community members share important values and a consciously chosen direction. Because they have received teachings together, they share a common language. They can speak to each other freely about deep feelings that are often harder to articulate with other people.

Most importantly, working together with the teacher, community members are developing capacities for openness, kindness and honesty. Spiritual community is a training ground, or gateway to expressing these wisdom virtues everywhere.

When we are participating in a spiritual community we are intimately relating to diverse people. These are the other students of the teacher, not people we hand picked. Members are often thrown together for long periods of time and are engaged in intense activities together. Within the context of a spiritual community, we are more committed to discovering the relaxation that allows us to experience compassion and devotion for everyone. Ideally, we take this with us when we leave.

It is easier to fool ourselves about our degree of realization when we are just doing seated practice on our own and then relating only to those we personally choose. Sometimes in this situation, it is our relations with our birth families that really show us where the karmic tensions are hiding!

Ideally, a spiritual community is doing its best to manifest the wisdom virtues of Shiva and Shakti. We are kind, welcoming hosts to all who encounter us. We are energetic and brave in our sadhana and daily life. We are spontaneous, adaptable and creative. And we are having a lot of fun!

A spiritual community should do its best to reflect what societies might be like if we were all a little more relaxed and aware. At the same time, the alchemy of a functioning Tantrik community magnifies, for its members the degree to which they are not yet able to fully manifest natural virtues. When we can see our karmic tensions more clearly, we are better able to work to relax them.

A functioning spiritual community is not just a collection of individuals. The teacher and lineage masters are the central channel of the community. The students become part of the energy body of the lineage. Vidya Shakti comes through the central channel for the benefit of everyone.

When the teacher does not hold the teachings and embody them with integrity, the body of the kula falls apart energetically and physically. The community becomes more of a parody, going through the motions and eventually disintegrating. Students should not be too concerned with this, as upsetting as it might be if you find yourself in such a community. Just pull up your stakes and move on.

Nothing is ever lost if you are using everything that happens to help you Self-realize. Kula is a specific manifestation of the body of the divine Mother designed to help people Self-realize. If you are a sincere student, Ma will always draw you into her kula.

Tantrik masters use communities in special ways to help members realize more quickly. You may find yourself constantly thrown in with someone who rubs you the wrong way, or continually pushed into situations that trigger your tensions. Plans may keep changing just when you thought you knew what was going on. You will find yourself to be both deeply challenged and relaxing to a degree you could not previously imagine.

As a kula or sangha member, your job is to remember the View and work to embody it in every situation. This does not mean that you try to act compassionate when you are really feeling crabby and selfish. It does mean that you try not to draw your spiritual family into your karmic drama.

Many of the practices people receive in Tantrik traditions are integrated. This means, you do them in the course of life, not on a cushion, or not only on a cushion. Taking responsibility for your reactivity within the context of community means remembering your larger purpose and invoking your practice right in the middle of your reactivity.

Karmic momentum entices you to reinforce your karmic grooves even more. When you are able to meet this momentum using the tools of your practice, the momentum shifts direction. If you do this over and over again, eventually the wisdom virtues of kindness and compassion naturally arise. You do not have to manufacture anything; you just have to relax.

PEOPLE SUCK

Let's cut to the chase. Whenever we deliberately try to hurt other people with anger, or when we angrily criticize ourselves, we are feeling self-hatred. I mean *every* time. No exceptions.

When you feel self-hatred, you may deal with it by lashing out at yourself or others. You might switch back and forth between other- and self-criticism. This is a depleting game of attack and withdraw.

Angry monologues can go on in your head much of the time even when they are not coming out of your mouth.

Anandamayi Ma never criticized anyone. Yet she was a fierce teacher who challenged her disciples to see and let go of their limitations. Criticism and clear-seeing are different. When you are being taught by a fierce teacher, you may be reactive, you may feel extremely uncomfortable, but you will always feel loved.

In the same way, you can have a clear view of yourself and others while still feeling self-love and respect.

People express their feelings of self-hatred in different ways, more or less internalized. Generally, though, the pain of self-hatred drives people to push the suffering outward. They project their bad feelings onto others and demand that other people, or external circumstances bear responsibility for their situation. It less painful to feel that *other* people suck.

If you tend to live at the projecting end of the spectrum, you probably have a running dialog in your head, or coming out of your mouth, about how other people screw up, piss you off, don't care, let you down, are stupid, arrogant, lazy and on and on. You might also ascribe your bad feelings about yourself to other people: They don't like me, are angry with me or don't appreciate me.

A young man I knew in a spiritual community was liked by all. He was quirky, but appreciated. However, he had adopted a self-concept that everyone rejected him. Even though no one was rejecting him, or perhaps *because* no one was rejecting him, he built a wall around himself and basically confirmed his self-concept by not speaking to others or joining in group activities.

The more he did this, the more isolated he felt, and the more strongly he was convinced that his situation was due to being rejected by the group. Some of us tried to intervene, but he had no capacity to self-reflect or receive nourishment. Eventually he left—a victim of his own karmic drama.

When we are stuck in this "hell," we start off lonely and feeling lack of self worth, and we end up pushing everyone away from both ends. We find fault and are certain people are finding fault with us. Then the situation self-destructs.

When we are strongly projecting this kind of karmic fixation, it is difficult to break away. We are convinced that we have a right to our bad feelings. Alternately, hopelessness can set in. We feel condemned internally and externally.

Fortunately, most of us have at least a little capacity to self-reflect and find the irony in our situation. With at least some capacity to receive the reflection of a teacher and laugh at ourselves, we can slowly loosen the grip of karmic vision and come to have more clarity.

Being a part of a supportive community of people on the same path is extremely important for people who are experiencing a lot of habitual, critical anger. They can try out new ways of relating within their communities and become less limited in their forms of self-expression.

Most importantly, people who live in an atmosphere of real and imagined criticism often have difficulty recognizing and accepting nourishment. You offer them a kind word, or a helping hand, and it is viewed with suspicion. As a teacher of mine says: *They turn water into fire.*

Over time, practicing in the crucible of a patient, honest and supportive spiritual community will help to open the prison gates of self-hatred. In our communities, we get to see everyone openly working with their own forms of suffering. We can laugh at ourselves. We start to recognize that we are all in the same boat. What a relief!

Coming to recognize that *we are all in this together* is a crucial first step toward experiencing our continuity with all of life. We may feel separate and alone, but our real condition is continuity. And this understanding *is* Self-realization.

THE LOWDOWN ON LINEAGES

Lineages are often defined as successive generations of teachers who hold and can disseminate the transmission energy of particular streams of teachings. This is one manifestation of lineage, but it is not the whole story.

Lineages are like rivers. Each river has a different character that meets the terrain and supports the ecosystems depending on it, yet all rivers are composed of nourishing water.

Just so, lineages are rivers of vidya Shakti flowing from the Supreme Self to teachers and on to students through time. Each lineage meets the unique needs of those who are bathing in its waters, and yet all true lineage nourishes the realization of continuity and the one taste of the creation.

Like the sustaining waters of Ma Ganga coursing down Shiva's locks of hair to moisten the parched land and slake the thirst of all beings, lineage is a supreme blessing. Those who sense her life, compassion and immense intelligence are eager to dive in.

Sometimes lineages flow through vast expanses of time, powerful and unbroken. Sometimes they manifest seemingly with no precedent as eternal teachings arrive in the human realm for an altered age.

Sometimes lineages hang on, having lost the capacity to transmit the vidya Shakti they once held. All manifest forms of lineage eventually resolve back to the unmanifest as new forms arise.

In order to be a teacher of the river, one must be a disciple of the river. This is the qualification. There is no real transmission without lineage, without the *abhisheka*, or blessing bath of the vidya Shakti of the divine Mother. All lineages are *Her*. All transmission teaching flows as a response to discipleship to Her.

Sometimes the transmission of lineage explodes; at other times it appears as a piercingly clear gem emerging from mist. Mostly, the flow of vidya Shakti is as a river: stately, implacable, yet playfully moving on, moving through, depositing understanding that is immediate and beyond any question of certainty or doubt.

I am not talking about a concept, or some transcendental subtlety. The reception of vidya Shakti is palpable, tangible and even shocking, or painful at times. You don't think it up, make it up, premeditate it or analyze it. It arrives.

The Guru-disciple process is what the Supreme Self has given us so that we can learn to surrender and discover natural devotion. Discipleship is the finest flower of natural devotion. Even the Guru bows to a true disciple.

When we discover natural devotion, we realize the devotion of the scent to the nose, the taste to the tongue, the touch to the body of the world. We discover that the entire world is puja or ritual worship. We can experience and understand directly that a lineage of teachings is the most exquisite devotional offering.

Teachers who take the seat of spiritual guide when they have no experience of discipleship, are perpetuating their own karma and the suffering of others.

To assume the role of a spiritual guide when one has only begun to swim in the shoreline eddies and flows of the river is risky because one might never leave that spot, or one might mistake the shoreline tide pools for the whole river.

Students sometimes devote themselves to teachers in order to make themselves feel safer or more important. Sincere teachers who do not yet have a real experience of discipleship can allow themselves to be lulled into fantasy by the fantasies of their students. Or they will even encourage these fantasies.

Committed discipleship to a teacher, to your own realization and to a lineage of teachings sooner or later strips you of fantasy. Over time, you will gain a good sense of how to work with your limitations, and so you will have something of value to offer others.

A sincere teacher who practices discipleship before all else has the opportunity to serve students well. Most teachers are not fully realized, but if they become great disciples, the river will flow.

SPIRITUAL UNTOUCHABLES

Spiritual communities are famous for clannishness, infighting and for harshly ex-communicating those who trouble other members of the group. In some instances, it is teachers who set the tone for this kind of activity. In other cases, the teacher is not around, and the fixations of the students are free to mask themselves with egoic mis-applications of the teachings.

A certain highly accomplished Guru traveled to a new city where some students had formed a group. Now, it so happened that, in the absence of Guru, one fellow had assumed the "top dog" leadership position in this group. He was enjoying his self-appointed role as the director of everything and everyone. In fact, he fancied himself quite an advanced practitioner capable of giving teachings to students even though he had no permission from the Guru.

This fellow was so attached to limited enjoyment he derived from this role-playing, he was like a heroin addict—compulsive and controlled by fantasy fixes. Far from being capable of leadership or conveying teachings to others, his display of confidence and knowledge was totally contrived. Others were impressed and followed along. They didn't know that acting "confident" and "knowledgeable" was just a part of the student's karmic programming.

So there this fellow was, playing the role of preceptor, when the real Guru showed up. The *faux* Guru didn't like the idea of being shut down. So he went into overdrive. He threw a tantrum and physically threw the real teacher out of the teaching hall and onto the street.

It was late at night and wintertime. The Guru had no place to sleep. But he was resourceful and luckily did not freeze to death! The next day, the Guru called a meeting. To everyone's surprise, he extended a kind invitation to the student who had thrown him out the previous evening. During that meeting, the clear seeing and compassion of the teacher acted like a reverse poison—a remedy. The student was freed of being possessed by his compulsion.

Without that compulsive programming, the real situation of the student could manifest. Far from being confident, he was terribly afraid that others might find out how unworthy he felt. Far from wanting to be the Guru, he longed with the grief of a little abandoned child for the Guru's love. But he felt so cut off from true love, he had tried to manipulate others into looking up to him, and even fearing him.

The spiritual literature of India, Tibet and many other places is filled with stories of accomplished teachers who encounter thieves, rapists, those possessed by greed, and even demons. With great insight and compassion, these teachers free other beings from fixation so that they too can continue on the path to Self-realization.

Students, all students, come to spiritual communities and teachers with their fixations, compulsions and attachments on full display. The student who is obviously disruptive is no more in the wrong or right than a student who tries to win the favor of the teacher with acts of false devotion and obedience, or one who uses "the teachings" as a weapon against other students.

If people didn't have fixations, there would be no need for teachers. In fact, Tantrik teachers are well-known for purposely inflaming the fixations of their students so that these may be recognized and resolved.

The greatest teachers neither seek nor reject students. All are welcome, without exception. However, this does not apply to every teacher. It only applies to those teachers who are Self-realized and can be of true benefit to the incredibly diverse beings they meet. The rest of us have to know our limitations and how these determine who we can benefit and who we cannot.

If a student is unteachable by a certain Guru, this is a reflection of the limitation of the Guru. So-called "bad" students should never be vilified by teachers or communities. We are all "bad" students until we are Self-realized. It is only a matter of degree.

This world, composed of nothing but intelligence and compassion, teaches everyone without exception. This is cosmic law. No one is unteachable. Only individuated teachers with their own limitations are not yet fit to serve everyone who comes their way.

Here are three golden rules for working with difficult situations within spiritual communities.

Treat any reaction you have to another person or situation as your reaction and your responsibility.

Your fixations are your karma; they are what you have to take responsibility for and work with. They are not caused by anyone else. The member of your community who really, really irritates you is, in a sense, your Guru. She makes sure that all of your attachments are visible. In reality, this person is none other than an aspect of World Self communicating with you.

Protect your practice.

We all have limitations. Being blind to these, or trying to rise above them with applications of spiritual View that you have not yet embodied, will slow your unfoldment. All students and most teachers, cannot encompass every situation. Sometimes we have to leave another person, or ask them to leave, or take some other measure to protect our ability to continue our practice individually or as a group.

The Buddha Yeshe Tsogyal once asked her Guru, Padmasambhava, what to do about disturbances to her practice arising in her environment. He answered that these disturbances should be brought into one's practice, "onto the path" as is said. But if this is not possible, his advice was: *Run for the hills! Protect your practice!* Notice that the emphasis is on what you should do to take responsibility for your sadhana, not on punishing, denigrating, criticizing or ostracizing another person.

The teacher is the teacher.

In the matter of the conduct of spiritual communities and a student's individual choices with respect to sadhana, the teacher is the guide and the arbiter. Students should ask the teacher what to do in difficult situations. Some students, in a moment when the watchful eye of the teacher is not on them, like to play the role of gatekeeper or even Guru. They try to wield power over other students, and this is the source of a lot of the bad reputation of spiritual communities. An accomplished teacher will know how to work with this situation so that everyone can grow. Put everything in the Guru's hands. Don't take on the karma of prematurely guiding other people, whether by giving them practices to do, criticizing them, or showing them the door.

Sometimes the most difficult student is transformed by interaction with the Guru into the most sincere disciple, an example to everyone. Even when students are in a fog of fixation and compulsion, they may be able to recognize the primordial light of insight and compassion shining from their teacher.

Even if you can't digest the behavior of a fellow student, hold a place in your heart for wishing that person well. Understand that everyone, absolutely everyone, will eventually realize. Never count anyone out.

TRANSFORMATIONS

The process of waking up will totally transform your experience, and yet you will remain what you have always been all along.

LIBERATION INCH-BY-INCH

PERHAPS YOU ARE somewhat disappointed, but you'll find no stories here of kundalini earthquakes, miracle healings or siddhas who walk through walls.

The stream of teachings you are encountering here is more like a workshop in somebody's backyard garage. As you walk by, you hear hammering and sawing, a bit of singing, and you wonder who is working so hard in there.

The fact is that when we read about amazing spiritual experiences, or tales of dramatic breakthroughs, what we often don't glimpse are the years of simple, consistent sadhana that brought those moments to fruition.

People with a high degree of openness (spiritual growth), have almost always done an enormous amount of practice. In fact, in the Tantras, the most prized aspect of human life is that we possess bodies that can do so many kinds of sadhana. According to the tradition, human life is the sadhana-doing-realm par excellence.

Despite the allure of amazing spiritual experiences and "sudden realization," the process of spiritual growth for ninety-nine percent of us proceeds in small steps. If you want to keep going, you need to learn to recognize and take daily pleasure in the infinite texture of this unfolding.

When I started practicing, I didn't know "Tantra" was the name for what I was doing. I didn't know from which country, or tradition the methods came.

Later, when I *did* know and had found a Guru and a kula, or spiritual community, I had no thought to measuring my accomplishments against those of others. I had no idea how my experience stacked up to anyone else's.

I also didn't read a lot of books detailing "amazing" experiences. I was more attracted to tales of disciples' devotion to their Gurus, and to the poetry and teaching texts of Kashmir Shaivism.

I was much more likely to compete for the emotional attention of my teacher than for siddhis, or marks of spiritual specialness. "Enlightenment" seem so lofty and far off, I hardly considered it. All I wanted to do was find out about Reality. This had been the driving preoccupation of my life.

I practiced *every* day. For years on end. For hours and hours a day. Through a natural process, and without planning, every moment of my life, waking, working and sleeping hours became sadhana.

It was through this steady, day-by-day, step-by-step process that some breakthroughs and miracles did occur, much to my surprise.

So, don't fret if you haven't yet come across the secret, all-in-one liberation pill that everyone knows about but you. Inch-by-inch is the way.

HOW TO USE A SPIRITUAL NAME

If you have a spiritual name, try to use it in your everyday life. Names are invocations. Each time a person says your name, they invoke the wisdom virtues inherent in that name. This is a transformative for you and for them.

My name is somewhat hard for people to pronounce. But I have noticed that when a person says it correctly for the first time, there is a broad smile. It feels good!

Whether your name is simple to say or more difficult, you do not want to make it even more challenging. Open the gates for everyone as much as you can.

Many initiates who live in English-speaking cultures, and now even in India, are given names that are spelled phonetically rather than in proper Sanskrit transliteration. This makes it easier for more people to feel comfortable pronouncing a spiritual name right away.

But of course, whatever way your teacher spells your name, that is how you should spell it.

Use your courage to bring your spiritual name into your everyday life. You will benefit from being reminded of your divine purpose and unique flavor wherever you are—at work, at play and while with your friends on the same path. If these happen to not be all the same thing for you, your spiritual name will unify your life.

For some people, the fact that we even have spiritual names is too challenging or upsetting. While it is an important part of your practice to use your spiritual name, your ninety-year-old grandfather from Romania who is very attached to family names is not going to benefit from your insistence.

Use your discrimination and self-reflection to decide when and how to use your name. The name should not become another source of gratification for small I. If you feel awkward using your name outside of your spiritual community, you can work with that tension.

Courage? Discrimination? Compassion? Relaxation? Your name is already teaching you these.

SPIRITUAL FANTASY OR SPIRITUAL GROWTH?

Am I experiencing real spiritual growth, or am I indulging in fantasy and wishful thinking? Every person doing spiritual practice should ask this question continually.

Spiritual awakening is the opposite of fantasy and trancing out. If you want to discover primordial awakeness and the fullness of human life, you must learn to recognize fantasy, and you must take steps to minimize opportunities to fall into fantasy.

Real spiritual growth is not a sensation, or a vision. It is not a cool dream. It's not even an initiation, or shaktipat. These phenomena sometimes open the door to spiritual growth, or signal that growth is possible, but *you* have to ground yourself in a good daily routine and consistent sadhana in order to transform a momentary experience into your new home base.

Growth means one thing: a bigger View. You learn more about who you are and Reality and you embody that.

In order to minimize the possibility of falling into fantasy, all practitioners must pay attention to what they eat and how they move and sleep. Why? Because it is easy to create disturbances in the body and mind and then mistake these disturbances for spiritual growth.

For instance, a raw food diet is one of the worst instigators of spiritual fantasy. In my experience working with students, it is impossible to progress spiritually if you eat only raw food. Yet so many people on a raw food diet feel that they are having elevated spiritual experiences. Why?

A raw food diet stirs up *vata*, or wind element to such a degree, a person may feel enlivened, excited or inspired. But it is more like soda pop fizzing in your energy channels. This kind of experience of liveliness is actually depleting in the long-run. It can even be mistaken for kundalini experiences by those who are ill-informed.

A raw food diet causes a misaligned relationship with space element and a lack of connection with earth element. You may feel very light, and even bodiless. Transcendental, cosmic-sized fantasies about yourself, the times, your band of friends, and so on can be provoked by this kind of diet.

The proof that raw food provokes fantasy is that most raw foodists cannot sit still comfortably for a seated practice and find meditation practice particularly hard. Their thoughts run wild, and they fall into trance states regularly.

They are dogmatically attached to their diet in the way that a person is attached to a mind-altering drug. When they do begin to eat cooked food again, depression can set in. Whatever they were experiencing was the result of the raw food and was not a level of realization at which they had truly stabilized.

Diet is powerful. Do your best to adhere to an appropriate diet and exercise routine, to guard against exhaustion and overstimulation and to get the right amount of sleep at the proper times. The goal is to properly calm and organize internal winds and relax the body and mind through appropriate conduct. This is the foundation of real spiritual growth.

Sometimes, through wrong View, a person misidentifies certain kinds of physical sensations as spiritual experiences. This happened to a teacher I know. He thought he was becoming enlightened when he was actually heading for a heart attack. So, taking care of the fundamentals of healthy conduct will ensure that you are less prone to taking these kinds of detours.

Another fundamental is working with an experienced teacher who has some realization and can guide you based on first-hand knowledge. My teachers have always asked me specific questions about the fruit of any practice I was doing, and they let me know when I was falling into wrong View, or fantasy. This is invaluable.

Some of my teachers have told me ahead of time about signs that a particular practice is developing correctly and bearing fruit. These signs, such as specific visions, insights or dreams, are called, in Tibetan, *nyams*. Nyams come from the experiences of Masters who have gone before us. We can all experience these same nyams because Reality has precise languages in which it communicates to us in our various circumstances.

Here are three of the most important signs of real spiritual growth.

Real awakening always shows up in day-to-day conduct. You will relate to people and situations differently.

If you have gained the fruit of a practice, you will embody the fruit, not just have some concept or fleeting experience of it. It may take quite some time to be able to integrate the relaxation and expansion we gain from practice into our everyday lives, but this is ultimately what real spiritual growth is about.

Spiritual growth is about more fully embodying the living, conscious wisdom of Reality.

When we experience real growth, we find we understand more about how Reality works. We can participate more fully based on this understanding. Spiritual experiences that remain, for us, on the level of physical or emotional sensation, are incomplete. They are good first steps, but we can know from this limitation that we still have a ways to go. Wisdom is the destination.

Once we have actually established ourselves at a new level, there is an impervious, vajra quality to that.

Maybe our human intellect still wants to brag, defend or doubt, but it doesn't get very far. In fact, our descriptions and explanations and arguments are just a joke. Real spiritual accomplishment is calm, self-luminous and self-evident. It doesn't need any dressing up or supports. It doesn't need to announce itself other than by showing up.

SADNESS AND SPIRIT

When we hold onto the idea that our practice must always be pleasant and must move us relentlessly toward feeling happier and happier, we suffer. We can feel anger, shame and frustration simply because we are experiencing the normal fluctuations of human life. The "happiness ladder" concept is one of the main obstacles to relaxation.

Pain and sorrow are part of the infinite palette of Shiva nature. Our relationship to these feelings changes as we relax, but life still displays itself through us in all of its colors.

At the same time, spiritual growth requires loss. No way around this. Each time we let go of tensions, while we will definitely enjoy the freshness of life in that state of greater relaxation, we will still grieve our "old self." We will, for a time, mourn our attachments to people, places, habits, and most of all, to the concepts that maintained our constructed sense of purpose and beliefs.

The world tells us when it is time to let go of the old, or simply takes it away at the proper time. Usually it tells us first, and then takes it away if we don't follow through on our own! We must listen very carefully, follow the hints and then work to relax into the new circumstance, which is bound to be somewhat scary at first.

When we are not fully letting go, we experience depression. While sadness moves us, depression is a state of energy stagnation. Depression that arises in the context of spiritual growth means that the new is arriving, but we haven't yet relaxed enough to fully embody it.

Don't bother analyzing your depression. Work directly with the stagnation. Try to do what you can to move your energy. Dancing, playing, singing, martial arts, yoga and adjusting your diet are all good choices.

The loss we experience as a result of growth must happen naturally. Continuing to do your practice during the dark times is key. This is how to "surf" through to the next level of relaxation even when the way is unclear and the waves feel overwhelming.

As more dogmas and fixations dissolve, or are ripped away, periods of destabilization and futile grasping for new ground are inevitable. While it seems paradoxical, if you can make the effort to relax at just these times and let everything unwind as it will without interference, you can enter into the experience of the natural, groundless state and discover the real meaning of refuge.

You will also gain tremendous confidence each time you go through the process of continuing to practice steadily even when you are feeling down and confused about whether you are making any progress at all. There is always a surprise at the other end.

The process of consciously working to relax and live in natural presence is not a linear path. We keep revisiting the different manifestations of our tensions as we go, although we will experience them differently than we did at some earlier point.

It is a cosmic law that there must be relative emptiness in order for the new to fully arrive. This is the part of spiritual life that requires extra bravery. You must let go of the old before you know what is ahead. Learning to surf the in-between is one of the most important spiritual capacities you will ever develop. When the new does begin to emerge, try to keep your focus on what is coming into your life, rather than on what you are losing.

KARMAKAZE

Tantrikas like to talk about "burning up karma." All sadhana burns up karma, but your average Tantrika wants to light a bonfire rather than a cozy, sandalwood-scented candle.

One way to burn up karma is to sit naked on a black rock in the desert, chant a few *crore* repetitions of a mantra and, out of pure compassion for all beings, let hungry vultures peck at you unimpeded. That'll burn some karma. Note: a crore is ten million.

Believe it or not, though, this is not the fiercest way. The fiercest way is to live totally without concern for karma. Place your entire life in the hands of Guru or God. Maintain the unbroken attitude that whatever happens is grace. Deal with the consequences of your actions without complaint or enthusiasm. Keep your head down and your awareness in a state of Guru yoga.

Obviously, this doesn't mean cultivate a numbed out state. It means maintain impeccable, awake detachment and devotion even when your world comes crashing down. No hope. No shame. No blame. No faking it! Become so at ease with any outcome, you slide between the karmic superstrings and watch them go *phffft* as you pass by.

Our first conscious encounter with karma is noticing the things we always do, aka our compulsive habits of body, energy and mind. We become more aware of the karmic patterns that compel our conduct. We might think about how those patterns manifest in our family, maybe even across multiple generations.

At some point, we go to an astrologer who gets us to think on a somewhat larger scale about the patterns that show up in our lives. Cosmic time, stars and planets enter the scene. But we are still indulging in the explanatory power of karma. Our astrology chart, nothing other than the record of our habitual activities in time, becomes another way to tell "the Story of Me."

Later, we might come to understand why the patterns that give our lives and our bodies a semi-predictable shape really don't belong to us: they start in infinity, end in infinity and touch everything along the way. The whole idea of karma as a collection of limited, personal knots blows up.

Then comes the part when we forget the story and actually feel the naked, push-pull force of karma as the world Self responds to our activities. This expansion of our View is overwhelming, but good medicine. If you are in this situation, you try to be more precise and appropriate in your actions. Karma is burning.

Some karmic tension feels yucky, some feels grand. But that's beside the point. All karma consists of consciousness and energy experiencing some kind of limitation, or some degree of ignorance of itself.

The world Self creates limited, patterned experience so that it can play the game of rediscovering its own limitless nature. You can understand this if you have ever enjoyed longing for an absent lover. Yes, you enjoy the longing and the reunion, both. That's the life process in a nutshell.

The unfreedom you are experiencing now is nothing but the result of the freedom of Shiva-Shakti to give rise to that limited experience. On a more individualistic level, your karma is the result of choices you freely made in the past. *Freedom is always more primordial than limitation.*

Some karmas are easier to relax than others. But you can always exercise what freedom you do have now to more consciously move toward Self-realization. However you choose, you will be contributing to either the hardening or unraveling of karmic limitations, not just for yourself, but for your ancestors, your children and everyone.

At the moment you are poised to make a choice such as "should I do sadhana today or slob around in front of the TV?", you can consider karma. How miserable do you want to be? How long do you want to take to relax and discover your real nature? And what do you want your experience to be next time around? (I hear from my sources there's a shortage of slugs in the slug realm.)

Each time that you consciously choose the habit of sadhana over the habits of more limiting karmas, you are taking another step toward releasing yourself from karma altogether and living a life of spontaneity and ease.

However, if you want to take the fiercest way, enter a state of continuous Guru yoga. Don't waver in your determination to be ever in a state of surrender to whatever life dishes up. Ignore your astrology. Discount everything I've said about karma.

Ready, set, go!

Warning: If you only pretend to be taking the fierce way, but really you just want an excuse to keep indulging your fixations, you'll end up entangling yourself in karmic tension even worse than before.

So, for those who aren't yet exactly ready for the karmakaze express, the advice is clear. Get help from good guides. Turn your limited resources to advantage through self-discipline. Eliminate karmic extravagance. Surrender your tensions through consistent sadhana. Exercise your out-of-shape freedom muscles and choose differently now, step-by-step. Allow karma to resolve in the course of your life. But still a little bit faster.

GHEE HAPPY

When the Dalai Lama first visited the United States, he was asked by an American Buddhist teacher about how to work with self-hatred.

> *Looking startled, he [the Dalai Lama] turned to his translator and asked pointedly in Tibetan again and again for an explanation. Finally, turning back to me, the Dalai Lama tilted his head, his eyes narrowed in confusion. "Self-hatred?" he repeated in English. "What is that?"* (qtd. in Salzberg)

Self-hatred is a powerful experience of separation from our true nature. We all feel some variety of this separation until we are Self-realized. However, some people have developed a greater capacity to "tune-into" Shiva nature, even in the midst of experiences of separation. Other people feel more overwhelmed by karmic tension and find it harder to take breaks from that.

Direct realization Tantra offers many tools that a person can use to work with these feelings and relax painful tensions.

But before talking about a couple of simple practices you can do if you are experiencing self-hatred, I want to make a distinction between working in a direct realization tradition and with typical forms of psychotherapy.

The usual kinds of psychotherapy in the West today proceed from a dualistic View. They don't question, and in fact tend to support, the belief that other people have caused your uncomfortable emotions.

Conventional therapy operates with the assumption that you can be fundamentally damaged by another. This keeps you in a state of fear and defensiveness, even if that fear goes underground during the "good" times.

In direct realization traditions, you learn that others do not cause your responses to life. This is proved by the fact that two people can be in the same situation, and one may feel victimized while the other may continue to feel that everything is fine.

Your response to a situation emerges from your unique karmic configuration.

Taking full responsibility for one's own responses in the world, without blame or shame, is radically emphasized over looking for external causes and solutions.

While therapists may highlight your heroic recovery rather than your victimization, in general, they do their best to support you in creating a more functional story about yourself: *the story of the strong self.* Most psychotherapy is based on affirming the individual self as a separate entity and upon telling stories about that self.

Direct realization practice is based on discovering connection and immediacy rather than on thinking about things and telling stories. A person who feels self-hatred and comes to work with a direct realization teacher will be asked to use the practice to discover a greater degree of natural exchange between themselves and their environment. This can be done through health cultivation, working with nature and sensory awareness, and ritual and service within a group context. There is much less emphasis on introspection for a person in this situation.

A person is not a discrete individual. The experience of individuality is a real experience, but individuality in the way we normally think of it is not our actual condition. Practicing yogis discover that there is only one continuous world with one body. This one body of consciousness and energy creates infinite styles of individualized experiencings.

Suffering arises when we mistake the *experience* of individuality for our primordial condition. The aim of direct realization practice is to be able to live in the world of diversity from the base experience of continuity rather than separation.

In the context of this View, there is no "other" to blame, and no individual "me" to hate. There is only God. When we begin to love Guru and God, we may not know it yet, but we are beginning to love ourselves.

There are two beautiful meditations from the Tantras that are simple and can be done by anyone. They will help you to begin to draw nourishment from your environment rather than continuing the tendency to experience others and the world as threatening.

First, you can make ghee, also known as clarified butter. Heat up some ghee each morning, and pour a few inches of the luminous, yellow liquid into a glass bowl. Then gaze steadily, but in a relaxed way, into the bowl each morning for 20 minutes. See what happens. Be sure to use organic butter. Don't use store-bought ghee.

You can do a similar meditation with a beautiful fresh flower. Put it on your altar at the height of your natural gaze. Sit about one foot away from the flower and gaze at it softly for twenty minutes each morning. Replace the flower as soon as any wilting appears. You can adopt either of these as practice for a month and see what happens.

The source of lasting self-esteem is the vajra pride, or adamantine pride that the Cosmic Self expresses in and towards its own creation. What we normally think of as self-esteem is an echo of vajra pride, and for this reason the best way to cultivate self-esteem for those at the beginning of the path is to begin to relax and de-identify with any stories you are carrying around about yourself or others. Then you can begin the process of re-identifying with the magnificence of the creation as evidenced in your very own body, in nature and in re-lationships with others. These two meditations will get you started.

REAL CHANGE

Change in our lives can look and feel very dramatic. You might move houses and jobs, find a new lover or totally remake your appearance. You might join a spiritual community, practice really hard and even have some spiritual experiences.

But if you are still operating with your same old story about yourself and the world, not much has changed.

People build defensive walls out of various karmic patterns. A defensive wall can be built of feelings of superiority, anger, pleasure-seeking, competition, holiness and so forth. Behind the wall is insecurity, fear and ultimately great loneliness.

It is possible to do sadhana from within a wall like this. It is possible to use spiritual life to make defensive walls even stronger.

I met a person who lived in an ashram and adopted orange robes even though he was not a *sannyasin* (a renunciate). He did a lot of karma yoga and was helpful to many people. On the other hand, he spouted nondual teachings all of the time, and these always had an aggressive delivery as if he were admonishing, or correcting people. He had no actual realization of the teachings; they had become servants of his defensive need to sound spiritually above it all. He was really just trying to avoid the pain of life.

Poignantly, every karmic tension is an attempt to resolve the pain of separation, at the same time that it ultimately keeps others at a distance. The recognition that you really want to connect is key to getting out of the prison of karmic fixation.

The job of the teacher and student working together is to bring down the walls and create the possibility of vertical change.

Real change is a change in View. This change is embodied. You feel different. You gain real, new insight into yourself and Reality. Your old story about yourself no longer feels appropriate or necessary.

Long-standing tensions resolve. Most importantly, your conduct changes. You literally become a different body because you are no longer identifying so strongly with small I and its boundaries.

Before we can experience real change, we must be willing to let go of some part of our story about ourselves so that fresh and new experience can touch us and remake us. This is the hardest part for most people. Why? Because we have to relax and let go before we understand or can see the leading edge of the new situation.

The willingness to surf the scary moments when we are in between the old and the new is gold for practitioners.

In direct realization traditions, the teacher challenges you in ways that, if you were to respond with openness, would lead to real change. This always entails giving up some cherished idea about yourself: what you must have, want or don't want.

We cannot take our fixations and tensions with us, try as we might. Eventually, we learn that only that which can and should fall away falls away. What is left is our primordial home in the Self.

GOING THROUGH SHAKTI TO MEET SHIVA

Shiva is an accomplished yogi. Shiva is a deity with many forms. Shiva is one possible name for Reality itself. Shiva is Lord.

How can we come to know Lord Shiva?

I once met a couple of practitioners who, when asked to describe their tradition, would answer: *We are finding TRUTH.* As they spoke these words, you could practically hear the capital letters. A funny little look would flit across their faces—a kind of "I dare you" gleam of self-pride in this supposedly ultimate and unassailable View.

The cosmos according to Tantrik View is not about truth or the getting of truth. The cosmos is simply expressive. As Swami Saty-ananda Saraswati said: *Truth is truth. I am not talking about truth. I am talking about Reality!* (Stevenson, DVD)

I like to use the example of a painting. You would not go up to a painting and declare: *This is true!* A work of art is neither true nor untrue; it is expressive. You might think it is poorly rendered, or brilliantly executed, but in either case, every painting is simply an expression. In this sense, all paintings are equal.

Manifest reality is the same. It is the expression of Lord Shiva. A better way of putting this is that manifest Reality is what Shiva nature naturally does. Our ordinary world is the life process of God.

Everything you see, hear, feel, touch, and taste, including yourself, is an expression of Shiva, made from Lord Shiva and is non-different from Shiva.

Every *loka* (realm) has its own flavor of expression. For instance, the flavor of the titan realm is jealousy. The flavor of Gandharva loka is music. Every class of beings perceives Reality differently because they are "doing" Shiva nature differently.

The infinite expressions we find in our world are aspects of the infinite potential of Shiva nature.

Imagine yourself enjoying a sporting event, or fighting with your mate or obsessing about your boss. Instead of indulging in unconscious immersion in these events, you might take a time out and think: *Hey, right now, I'm an aspect of Shiva's infinite potential expressing itself. How interesting!*

Or wherever you are now, take a moment to enjoy one of your five senses and experience that as part of the unique cosmic personality expression we call "human." Feel that you are Shiva nature enjoying its creation through the gateway of your senses.

When you meet someone who turns you off, or on, you can try viewing that person as You (Shiva) with a different personality display.

When we allow ourselves to experience the variations we encounter as creative expression, this helps us to shift our experience from the drama of attachment to the relaxation and smoothness of enjoying the world just as it is.

Many traditions teach that there is an ultimate reality, or truth that exists elsewhere, for instance, in heaven or Brahma Loka. These traditions are called "transcendental" because the goal of the practices they teach is to transcend the world we experience every day.

In the tradition of Kashmir Shaivism, *this* world is no different from the ultimate reality. In fact, there is only one Reality expressing itself in myriad ways, and they are all God.

What we are dealing with is not being in the wrong place, but our limited View of *this*.

One of the most important teachings in the entire Kashmiri tradition is that if you want to know the Lord, you must come to know *this*.

Shakti is Lord Shiva's creative power. This world, your ordinary world right now, is Shakti, the creative energy of Lord Shiva creating and appearing as this fantastical display of infinite variety.

As it is said in the tradition: to know Shiva, you must know Shakti. There is no understanding of Shiva apart from Shakti.

Shakti is the body, the personality and the life process of the Lord. Simply put, it is the nature of the Lord to create, destroy and maintain *this*. Our world *is* the nature of God.

In the Tantrik traditions, we practice with all of the aspects of our lives. The wonderful fact is that we can practice with the elements with our everyday life and become Self-realized because all of the Lord's creations *are* the Lord.

We are not trying to escape because there is nowhere to go. What we *do* want is to relax our limiting karmic vision so that we can have a fuller and more direct encounter with the nature of God, our own nature, here and now.

THE DARK DREAM

In a famous novel of the early '70s, characters are said to be "on the Dark Dream."

"He won't bother us for a while," They tell each other. "I just put him on the Dark Dream." (Pynchon 697)

The Dark Dream is addiction to knowledge, command and control. Basically, the Dark Dream is everything that normal Western culture values and for which it compulsively and competitively strives.

We are told we can exercise command and control over our lives, nature, biology, other people and nations. We are trained to monomaniacally seek limited, mechanistic knowledge and intellectual understanding.

The fundamental reason why, as Tantrikas, we must wean ourselves from the Dark Dream is this: Reality is simply not open to the kind of knowledge, command and control small I has been taught to desire.

Paradoxically, the only way small I can achieve a measure of satisfaction and personal power is by remaining in a state of ignorance. If you notice, the word "ignorance" contains the word "ignore."

We can only convince ourselves that we have achieved mastery when we ignore whatever falls outside of our domain. And there is always an outside because Shiva nature is infinite.

Of course, we can learn to do things such as create breathtaking art, perform surgery and build bridges. We can cook beautifully, and some great yogis among us will even be able to walk through walls, or appear in two places at one time.

But whenever small I is perpetuated through attachment to "powers," those powers are fundamentally based on ignorance. We may have know-how, but we lack wisdom.

The infinite, devotional heart of realization always escapes those who are themselves limited by the desire to control or capture life.

In India, Tantra is often associated with magic and with people who can wield special powers over others and the forces of nature. Some of the lesser Tantras, or ancient written teachings, contain nothing but formulas for exercising one's power, usually to get money, sex, love, status and revenge. These "teachings" are not about Self-realization, although as is true of similar "Tantra" teachings today, they likely attracted paying students!

The living awareness that outruns capture and overflows concepts, while powerful indeed, has no ambition or attachments. It has no reason to do or not do anything, other than awake, spontaneous, playful self-expression. This Self is your real refuge. To more fully embody it is your birthright and inevitable destination. Dedicating yourself to a practical wisdom tradition such as Tantra is the way to get there.

The compulsion to know, command and control is a defensive posture of small I. It is the deepest, most entrenched tension each of us will encounter in our practice. This aggressive defensiveness, and its underlying root fear, is what we must surrender.

But the world Mother is generous. She gives us opportunities galore to surrender our defensiveness. We have various ways of describing these opportunities: failure, trauma, reactivity, loss, getting our buttons pushed, not getting what we want, what we think we are owed, or what we expect.

Every time we encounter one of these moments, we have a choice: let small I mount its familiar, frantic attempt to plug up the leaky containers of our lives, or recognize that bottomless feeling for the opportunity it is and consciously relax, opening to a more immediate encounter with livingness.

Moments of high defensiveness and reactivity are skin-close to the free fall of surrender. If you consciously choose to relax right in the midst of high tension, right at peak moments of fear, anger, resentment, shame and so on, you will enter directly into the root fear, then the root void, and then, finally, you will rediscover openness, liveliness, and compassion.

Such moments can also arise when we are moved by the sky-like condition of our teachers. Given the right circumstances, the alchemy between student and teacher can also catapult you out of the prison of small I and into the encounter with life.

On the other side of the Dark Dream, you will find the confidence and spaciousness to adapt to life's ever-changing circumstances. You can be naturally responsive rather than defensive and reactive.

Have I convinced you to try it? Aw, come on! It's either that, or the Dark Dream.

MAGIC AND GRACE

The highest Lord is always intent on creativity through his Shakti. He showers grace, manifests and withdraws without any restraint (for grace only). — Trikahrdaya (qtd in Abhinavagupta, A Trident of Wisdom 14-5)

GET REAL MAGIC

THE DIFFERENCE IN View between my students here in the U.S. and many of those who write to me from India is dramatic.

Folks who write from India usually assume that I have powers such as clairvoyance and the ability to predict the future. Some have it in mind that I am a particular favored goddess. I have been asked for mantras to manifest deities and kill annoying neighbors.

If right at this moment, whether from your comfortable seat in India or elsewhere, you are chuckling and appreciating your own greater sophistication, read on!

Here in the U.S., I have to stuff skeptical students full of stories about the magic of the world. I tell them about accomplished human beings who walk through walls, become invisible, receive transmissions of complex practices out of "thin air" and who actually *do* see far off people, places and things as if they were in the same room.

I try to impress upon my students that the sounds of kundalini running in the channels of a human body are more captivating than any rock concert, that the lights of the five elements are more entertaining than the latest science fiction blockbuster movie and that just being in the world in a relaxed and natural way is a higher high than that offered by any drug.

I watch their faces and often see a mixture of uncertainty, cool cynicism and longing.

Despite all of our whiz-bang technology, here in the U.S., we live in a culture that is almost devoid of any comprehension of Real Magic. What do I mean by Real Magic? I mean the fullness of Reality, particularly as demonstrated to us by someone in a human body.

Our parents, by and large, have not brought us up with tales of human beings who embody more of Reality than we can readily imagine. When we meet a human who has realized a fuller humanity, we label that person a God, or a saint or crazy. We rarely allow ourselves to admit the possibility that a spiritually accomplished person is an ordinary human being who has demonstrated constancy and capacity in regular old spiritual practice.

Most people in the U.S. do not actually know a single person of spiritual accomplishment. If we did, we might have more confidence in ourselves and the process of awakening.

Sometimes when we do meet a Guru, or even just a yoga teacher, we can be ridiculously over-earnest and exaggerated in our displays of devotion. We don't know how to relate, so we fake it by over-dramatizing, even fooling ourselves much of the time.

These displays are a result of our longing for it all to be real and of our inability to relax and let Reality show us the way. Our underlying lack of confidence in the process and promise of Self-realization gets in the way even as we are prostrating earnestly to our chosen One.

Or we keep trying to reason, compare and contrast our way through every encounter with spiritual teachings and teachers, starving ourselves of real spiritual nourishment.

The fact is that most of what we relegate to the category of wacky stories about spiritual adepts—those stories we suspect are products of ignorant, gullible cultures—are actually more real than all of the crap we believe.

Like that the world is solid, made up of distinct objects, explainable by scientific methods, and fixable by the right combination of life coaching, psychotherapy, designer pharmaceuticals and cosmetic surgery.

Recently, I met an older yogini from Tibet. She told me that, in Tibet, she never revealed to students what practices she had completed, nor did she make a display of her experiences or accomplishments. Here, she says, she is more likely to do these things because students need it. She is acting out of compassion, not egoism.

Even when students in the West find an accomplished teacher, they sometimes cannot relax, receive transmission, or take the time to let spiritual practice develop. They don't have any confidence in Real Magic. They are starving amidst plenty.

I always hope students will see me as an ordinary person who has practiced for a bunch of years and has realized some of the fruits of that practice. First of all, this is the truth. Second of all, I want students to feel greater confidence in the process of life and the teachings of the tradition. If I tell them about some of the more "amazing" events in my life, it is not to appear special, but precisely because I am *not* special. If I can experience these things just by doing ordinary, consistent sadhana, so can anyone.

When you allow yourself to have confidence in the teacher, the teachings, Reality, or yourself, you can relax and let yourself be carried along. You can be more open and exploratory. Then the real magic of life can appear before you, as you.

You don't need to rid yourself of doubts. Doubting is a soft and open position. You do need to let go of the brittle blinders of skepticism.

Take a look around. Find a teacher in whom you can see your real potential as a human being. Don't compromise on that. Then you can discover Real Magic for yourself.

GIMME A PEAK

Many people desire to have a peak experience that will soften their feelings of isolation. We search for these peak experiences in sex, food, drugs, religion, in our spiritual practice and from our Gurus.

People of all faiths, and even atheists, long to be saved.

The desire to be saved attracts a lot of people to lineages in which teachers promise miracles, or give shaktipat. This desire fuels attachment to stories of amazing spiritual feats. It causes people to look for quick fixes, and when they do settle into a practice, it causes them to indulge in fantasies of obtaining sudden enlightenment, or special powers. People can become spiritual experience junkies just as they can become sugar or heroin addicts.

The desire for peak experiences is the same desire that will eventually lead to Self-realization. There is wisdom in this desire. People want to be saved from the pain of separation, the root ignorance. They want to be pushed over the edge of limitation.

But seeking miracles, or simply wanting someone else to cause us to become enlightened, is only a stage along the way. Such limited desires are mostly abandoned as we discover more confidence in our own essence nature: unconditioned consciousness and energy.

At this point, we can begin to take more responsibility for our Self-realization. We become capable of working with a teacher and of relating to the teachings in a more mature way. We develop a higher capacity for self-reflection, and our reactivity to the circumstances of our lives begins to diminish.

We work very hard. We are really on the path. Now we desperately desire to fully unfold within ourselves the courage and capacity to discover our real nature.

This is also a stage—perhaps thousands of lifetimes long. It is the stage of hard sadhana.

At some point, though, our desperation begins to soften. We find ourselves in less of a life and death struggle with our fixations. We discover a new sense of intimacy with all life. The distinctions between "inside" and "outside" begin to dissolve. We no longer experience our teachers or other wisdom beings as radically different from ourselves. When we hear the voices of our teachers, we hear our own wisdom speaking to us.

Eventually, we realize that the entire world is a living communication of Self to Self. There is nothing to pursue or collect. The "I" we thought was on the road to being rewarded for all of that hard work is discovered to be itself a limitation.

The understanding dawns that there are infinite factors involved in the process of waking up. Our activities are important, but devotion and surrender are more so. We are letting go of even the identity of "yogi," or whatever our spiritual identity happens to be. Attachment is just attachment, and any attachments will hold you back. Even the attachment to conceiving of yourself as a "practitioner."

When I finally read Yogananda's *Autobiography of a Yogi* at the age of forty-five, I was deep in the stage of effortful sadhana. I felt desperate for insight into the nature of Reality, my nature. I am talking about real desperation. The kind that hurts your heart and leaves you gasping for breath.

What struck me about the story most occurred near the end. The narrator is granted visions of accomplished beings who have moved on to other, non-earthly realms and who are still doing sadhana to help them unwind remaining karmas (352-69).

I felt, not excited, but a sense of horror. Was I going to be at this for eons? Painstakingly untying the knots in age after age, realm after realm?

Now, however, the feeling of separation has softened. I find it impossible to experience the life process as so burdensome. I no longer experience horror at the thought of myself soldiering on alone toward enlightenment. Not that I am enlightened, mind you. I'm just not so much of an "I" anymore—not a soldier—not alone. And so there is more humor and less horror.

In my earlier years, I tried to push through to greater realization. Now I am listening. I am using my freedom to follow life, to follow Nature, to follow the promptings of wisdom even, or especially, when they lead me away from where small I thinks it wants to go.

AMAZEMENT AND THE DELIGHT OF EXPERIENCING

Reflect on the fact that experiencing exists. Just this fact. The fact of experiencing is at least as interesting as what is experienced.

Usually, we obsess about "my experience," or "having experiences." But for now, just contemplate the state of experiencing. The state of experiencing doesn't belong to any one individual.

The manifest world is Shiva's theater of experiencing.

A person who has a high degree of realization is simply enjoying, or delighting in the infinite varieties of experiences that embodied life affords. The *Siva Sutras* describe this person as wonderstruck, or in a state of joy-filled amazement (Lakshmanjoo 44).

Abhinavagupta defined our human senses as deities playing in the field of duality (*A Trident of Wisdom* 38-40).

The Maharastrian poet-Siddha, Jñanadeva, wrote: *The non-dual one enters of his own accord the courtyard of duality. And the unity deepens along with the growth of difference (Amritanubhava 85).*

What these teachings have in common is the insight that the Supreme Self delights in exploring his own nature through the myriad sensory experiences he imparts to the infinite beings that are his own creation and his own body.

Even ordinary amazement leads us outside of small self-concept. The expression of amazement says it all: eyes wide open, mouth ajar, no self-referencing thought. The spontaneous expression of amazement and the facial posture of nonconceptual meditation are identical.

Amazement short-circuits attachment to thoughts; it opens a gateway to nonconceptual awareness. Amazement literally blows your ordinary, karmic mind so that primordial wide-awakeness can surface. Those who have deeply relaxed, shedding their karmic fixations, abide continuously in this natural state of awake, wondrous experiencing.

The ultimate attachment from which we suffer is the attachment to holding onto experiences. Attachment to experiences is the most gross and most subtle hindrance to Self-realization.

Holding onto experiences actually blocks us from becoming immersed in the endlessly flowing river of experiencing. And yet our attachment to having experiences is still an echo of Shiva's enjoyment of the creation.

This is why beginner Tantrikas are often given the most easily enjoyable practices and are likely to be found adorning their altars and participating in lavish rituals. Teachers use the attachment to pleasure and beauty in order to get students more attached to sadhana. Later, these gross pleasures are not so necessary.

After we clear out the gross attachment to experiences, the more subtle layers become tangible. These layers consist of "experience reflexes."

The experience reflex keeps attempting to grab onto the flow of experiencing, stabilize it and possess it. Even when there is no story, or very little story left, small I has a habit of picking at the state of experiencing like someone nervously picking a thread out of a whole cloth.

It's really annoying, until it becomes funny.

At some point, this compulsive picking reveals itself as an expression of our fear of change and death. When you stop grabbing, categorizing and embalming experiences, when you open out into the state of experiencing, you also begin to lose your grip on linear time.

Linear time is time marked and chunked by the drama of "my experience" and "having experiences." Most of us have experienced losing track of time while on a vacation. When we are totally immersed in the living presence of experiencing, linear time disappears.

The world of "my experiences" versus the state of experiencing is the difference between walking around in fifty pound gravity boots on ice and jumping out of a plane. This is one of the reasons why Tantrik sadhana often features jumping from high places. When we do things that are scary and exhilarating, we encounter something like the amazing pure presence of experiencing without past, future or ordinary present time.

CASTING A SPELL

Did you ever notice that "spelling" means both a magical act and the act of correctly ordering letters in written texts? In our modern context, we have learned to relate to books and language merely as vehicles to convey information. We have lost our connection to the magical, "spelling" capacity of language.

The idea of language as mere representation, or information is far from the Tantrik View in which language is fundamental to reality and the process of creation. Reality itself is composed of communication. As Tantrikas, we learn to relax and open to the magical force of language and its active transmission of vidya Shakti.

This is a vast topic, and a fascinating one. What follows is a brief map of the Tantrik cosmos and the word.

Paravac is the Supreme Word, the primordial throb or vibration of consciousness that ultimately gives rise to worlds. Paravac is the source of creation and the infinite potential within all creation.

Paravak is the Supreme Goddess of the word, the Divine Mother or Adi Shakti.

Pashyanti is Shakti manifesting as the desire of the Supreme Self to experience its own infinite potential. This desire impels the ever on-going creation of worlds of experience.

Madhyama is Shakti manifesting as silent mental articulation.

Vaikhari is Shakti manifesting as audible speech.

What we experience as solid reality emerges at the endpoint of a cascade from subtle to gross vibratory experiences. At the most subtle point is what is called "visible sound," or the light of consciousness. From this emanates the subtle forms of the letters of the Sanskrit alphabet and the mantras that seed duality.

The cascading movement from paravak to vaikhari is expressed by the understanding that Ma Sarasvati, the Goddess of speech, dances on the tongue of the Guru or adept. The words of the teacher are none other than Ma Shakti herself. So listen up!

This is also why students are often admonished to avoid unnecessary speech. Wasting speech is literally wasting or misusing the divine Shakti.

Mantras are the direct sound forms of cosmic wisdom virtues. When we do sadhana with mantras given to us by our teachers, the wisdom virtues of those mantras are directly revealed to us. Some mantras have translatable meanings, and some do not. If a mantra is translatable, knowing the translation of the words is helpful, but practicing the mantra with the correct orientation and View is paramount.

One form of mantra practice is the writing of mantras either on paper or on the body. This common sadhana orients us toward greater understanding of the continuity of the body of words with our literal bodies.

We come to understand that we are spoken, or spelled into existence by Ma Shakti.

Perhaps the greatest demonstrations of the textual nature of Reality is the emanation of received texts, or treasure texts as they are called in the Tibetan traditions. Treasure texts are teachings that arrive spontaneously and fully-formed in the minds, dreams and environments of great teachers. They are transmitted directly from wisdom itself, sometimes through *dakinis*, or female subtle beings whose job it is to relay teachings into the human realm.

Vasugupta was a Kashmiri devotee of Lord Shiva. He lived at the end of the ninth century and the beginning of the tenth. Out of compassion for human beings, Lord Shiva appeared to Vasugupta in a dream and told Vasugupta to search for a teaching on the nature of Self—*The Shiva Sutras*—engraved underneath a rock on Mahadeva Mountain.

Vasugupta set off to find Lord Shiva's transmission, and indeed it was exactly as the Lord had described in the dream. Vasugupta simply touched the rock and, as it turned over, the text appeared and was transmitted directly into Vasugupta's mind. Vasugupta spent the remainder of his life disseminating these timeless teachings which are still with us today (Lakshmanjoo, *Shiva Sutras* 10).

A hundred years earlier in Tibet, the Buddhas Padmasambhava and Yeshe Tsogyal hid thousands of teachings in rocks, mountains, and lakes and in the minds of the unborn. Their reason for doing so was greatly compassionate. They felt that, in the future, humanity would be in need of fresh teachings to guide us through dark times. They were able to do this because the nature of Reality is fundamentally communicative, comprised of intelligence and power.

The treasure texts of Padmasambhava and Yeshe Tsogyal are still being discovered by adepts today who are able to access Reality at these profound levels. The discovery of treasure texts is still showing us that the world, teachings and texts are just different modes of appearing of the same interwoven Reality.

A teacher whose tongue or pen is dancing with vidya Shakti, who can "spell" correctly, is a vehicle for transmitting the energy of understanding to many students through both oral and written speech. However, for the catalyst of vidya Shakti to work through our lives, we must listen and read differently from how we are taught in school and by our cultures at large.

We must listen and read in an open, relaxed state, resisting the temptation to accumulate knowledge based on limited, prefabricated understandings. We must read with our hearts, the true seats of wisdom, and not so much with our conceptual, judgmental, acquisitive minds. We must read, and listen, in an original way, alive to the fresh spelling of Reality in every moment.

WHAT IS GRACE?

> *It has to be admitted that everything happens as a result of one's actions. As everyone acts, so he reaps the fruit. However, at a certain stage the aspirant becomes aware of God's grace, then he declares that nothing at all happens without grace. But in actual fact, it is due to the result of his own actions that he has earned the privilege to become the recipient of Divine Grace.* —Anandamayi Ma (*Ananda Varta*, 28.3: 172-3)

We all have expectations of ourselves, others and the world that are based on our tensions—on our limited View of what is possible for us and life.

Someone suggests: *Why don't you try this new way of doing things?* Another person might habitually answer: *Oh no, that will never work!*

This is an example of a common kind of limitation of View, aka ignorance of Reality. The person wonders why new opportunities never seem to arise when it was she refusing them day after day.

We have entrenched Views of ourselves and others such as: *I'm always getting the short end of the stick!*, or *He's so manipulative.*

We are so enslaved by our limited View, we don't even notice when life surprises us, or we quickly dismiss something that doesn't fit our story. We actually enjoy getting right back to our miserable outlook. We condemn ourselves and others to narrow, painful roles in life.

In this condition, we are, as has been written in the scriptures, like jars with the lids on. No new nourishment, or learning can get through to us.

When we begin to practice in a spiritual tradition, we slowly soften our self-image defending stance. We start to notice more about ourselves, and eventually, more about other people. The world begins to come alive again. Skepticism, negativity and anxiety start to be relieved by moments of relaxation, natural enjoyment of what is, confidence in life and even wonder. We begin to understand more about how the totality of Reality works—about natural law.

In this new condition, brought about by consistent effort in sadhana, we can notice life responding to us, assisting us to Self-realize, even clearing the path so that we can continue with renewed dedication and desire.

A student of mine recently had this experience. She was involved in a situation with another person that had been stuck for quite some time. Her View was that she couldn't do anything but continue to be entangled.

She was already projecting her negativity a year into the future, when she was certain that she would not be able to go on a planned pilgrimage to India with me because of her entanglement with this other person.

However, through her sadhana and listening to the teachings, she gained much more clarity about her role in keeping the entanglement going, and she gained enough detachment to resolve to change her behavior in a significant way. Still, karmic tensions were expressing as a certainty that the other person would respond badly to her desire to go to India with me.

What happened instead was that the other person, upon hearing her new clarity and resolve, did something "surprising." He offered to pay for her trip. Now this student has more opportunity to practice and more confidence in life.

This is one aspect of grace. We experience a sudden opening to a new level of opportunity that comes about as a response to our effort.

The natural fact is that when we are 100 percent ready to resolve some karmic tension, that is entirely the same as God being 100 percent ready. Self responds to the Self-surrender of Self.

That we are rarely 100 percent ready to give up our attachments to habit is why Self-realizing takes so darn long! But it is also why it could take only an instant.

When we start to relax, we more and more notice how life supports us to Self-realize. This "support" can come in the form of challenges, obstacles and restraints, but it is all grace. Whatever happens has the potential to move us in the direction of realization.

Other aspects of the human experience of grace can be more spectacular. These are the kinds of manifestations of spiritual accomplishment that you read about, or perhaps have experienced yourself. A teacher gives a mantra in a dream. Or an "incurable" illness is resolved through prayer. Or you experience a time when a more realized condition visits to show you the way. Or you meet your real teacher. That is supreme grace.

Whatever it is, you can be sure that you are being responded to because of your readiness. Now, having that response, it is time to work harder so that you can stabilize the insights and effects of that experience. An experience of grace is never a culmination. It is an invitation to realize more and a new beginning.

CONSTANT CONVERSATION

Duality is a theater of communication. Relax the boundaries of your senses, and you will learn to participate in the ceaseless dialog, the unbroken call and response of Reality.

CONSTANT CONVERSATION

ONE DAY, A visiting doctor came to say goodbye to Anandamayi Ma. His train for Bombay was departing that afternoon. A devotee stood combing Mataji's long hair. Mataiji suggested that the doctor take a different train, but the man was in a hurry and could see no logic in this.

Without looking at him, Ma plucked a few strands of hair from the comb. She wound them three times around the middle joint of her index finger with great precision. Then she said very slowly, *Everything I say . . . , and every thing I do has . . . meaning* (Lannoy 24).

When people talk about the meaning of life, they generally want to discover what makes life important. Or, if they are speaking about the meaning of their own lives. The idea of permanency is also mixed up with the idea of life's meaning. People want to leave a mark on life, or they want life itself to be headed toward some kind of ultimate "solution" to the "problem" of life.

From a Tantrik perspective, life has no meaning in the conventional sense. Instead, life is expressive, communicative and responsive. The person undertaking Tantrik sadhana discovers that Shiva nature expresses itself with delight. The "meaning" is simply the enjoyment of *that*.

Expressions are always communications. We can only communicate when there is some sense of an other to whom we speak. The capacity of the world to appear in the form of different beings allows for the experience of communication. Duality is the expressive theater of Lord Shiva.

Communication is by no means limited to sentient beings. The entire world is participating. The flowers are expressing themselves to the nose. The patterns of bird flight to the wind. The sun to our entire world. These are not metaphors.

Communication launches itself in an infinite network of reception and response. As we go along in our sadhana, we discover the response of the world to our communications. We discover that we are living in a rich field of communication.

A common way that we begin to participate consciously in the seamless field of Reality's communication is through ritual. Once we learn the correct ritual language, and when we are able to relax into an open, communicative state while performing ritual, we can begin to notice the powerful responses that ritual evokes. This can be quite shocking for Westerners who are used to performing rituals with a bit, or a lot, of skepticism.

Whether or not you enjoy ritual, if you practice consistently, you will begin to speak the language of the world more precisely. You will develop precision in your activities as you get more in tune with the tune of Reality.

When Anandamayi Ma declares that everything she says and does has meaning, She is speaking directly on behalf of Reality. She is letting the young doctor know that his narrow, ordinary reasoning is blocking his understanding of his real situation.

In Anandamayi's world, all of life is a meaningful communication. In the doctor's world, only "logical" statements or a limited range of other expressions are "meaningful." Perhaps he might also notice "coincidences."

The doctor is a barely literate person, while Mataji speaks, reads and writes all of the world's primary languages.

If you happen to meet any highly realized persons, it is often the case that they appear to be listening to signals near and far. Such a person's senses extend through time and space. When we relax, we too can join the multi–dimensional flow of constant conversation.

THE PRECIOUS WORDS OF MY TEACHER

Up until I reached my late thirties, on certain days the colors, textures, sounds and movements of the world felt painfully intense. Sometimes I couldn't bear to go out into nature because the brilliant liveliness of nature overwhelmed me. Only after I had done years of Tantrik sadhana could I digest these experiences.

I remember one day when on a camping trip with my diksha Guru, I confessed to him that, for the first time, I felt totally relaxed while out in nature. He looked at me with genuine shock.

As people practice, they relax and experience more of Reality. Colors become more luminous, and all of the senses begin to sharpen. This can be disturbing if you are used to living in a fog. Far from encouraging the withdrawal of the senses, or trance or benumbed states, Tantra promotes expansion of the senses and alertness to the precise communications of the world.

This communicative precision of the world Self expresses itself in the words and actions of accomplished teachers. Students will often say how mysterious it is that the teacher should talk about exactly what has been on their minds in some moment. But most of the time, the teacher is not reading your thoughts! Nothing that deliberate need take place.

The teacher's words are simultaneously addressing the concerns of *many* students even though students are in different conditions. This is because the open state of the teacher allows for more cosmic "bandwidth." Her words emerge naturally and spontaneously in response to the precise situation of whoever happens to be around. This is an important lesson that the Guru spontaneously teaches us about how Reality works.

Many of my teachers have been exceptionally precise with words. Anandamayi Ma was a consummate communicator. She was able to speak simultaneously in ways that touched people in extremely different circumstances, from the illiterate to the pandit, from the ignorant to the accomplished siddha.

The world Self communicates precisely through great teachers, but students, in general, do not yet have the capacity to be precise listeners.

When we are relatively ignorant, i.e., stuck in duality, we tend to paint the world with the broad strokes of our concepts and fears. We want a manageable world, a familiar world that we can grasp as easily as possible. We grasp at the world instead of letting it communicate to us in its own way.

Many people, upon listening to the precise words of the teacher, have a tendency to turn those words into something familiar.

We may feel happy, thinking we hear the teacher affirming our pet fixations. Or we may become upset, believing that the teacher has made some terrible mistake, or has attacked us. In many cases, our fears and insecurities have caused us to imprecisely listen to the teacher's words.

At the same time, because we have agreed to be in a teaching situation, we slowly begin to experience more of the picture. After hearing the same thing repeatedly, the real import of the words begins to sink in. Other times, of course, words are heard immediately, and the opening is immediate also.

Anandamayi Ma compared the flow of the words of the wise to water dripping on stone. Eventually, the water creates a hole.

> *By listening repeatedly to discussions and discourses on topics of this kind, the path to first-hand knowledge of what has been heard gradually opens out. You know, it is as when water uninterruptedly dripping on a stone finally makes a hole in it, and then a flood may sud-*

denly surge through which will bring Enlightenment.
(Words 3)

Receiving transmission teachings about your real nature is relaxing. Holding onto your fixations and ideas about the world is a lot of work. When you let your ideas and fixations go, it is as if a heavy knapsack has dropped from your shoulders. You can put down your burdens and rest.

The way to receive the transmission of the precise words of a teacher is to relax and open all of your senses. Don't just use your legal mind, or your emotional drama mind. Listen in a total way. Let yourself be moved. Don't worry about not understanding all of the teachings. If you let go and relax, whatever needs to sink in will do that.

Arguing with the teacher is, of course, the path that some people take, especially in the West. And arguing is sometimes, but not always, an aspect of listening closely. Any path is ok, as long as there is also a conscious kernel of willingness to let go and surrender to your innate desire for realization. In order to realize the fruits of a student-teacher situation and receive the teacher's precious, precise words, any fixation has to be tempered by a certain level of aware responsiveness to this simple, heartfelt desire.

KARMA AND MERCY

Karma means action. But it is specifically action performed with limited View. Until we are Self-realized, our experience is more or less governed by ignorance and attachment. We can exercise our freedom to varying degrees, but we often choose to follow the momentum that we ourselves gave generated by cultivating attachments to objects, admiration, success, love, drugs, food, emotions, likes, dislikes and so on. We can call this momentum compulsion and addiction. But mostly we believe these karmic patterns are "who I am."

When we talk about "my karma," good or bad, we are really talking about the appropriate response of Nature to our activity in the world. If we eat improperly, we get sick. Our emotions and mind become unbalanced. If we spend money improperly, we get into financial trouble. If we are angry and rude, people won't want to spend time with us. This is the simplest way of understanding karma, but of course there is more to it than these simple examples.

Karma does not refer to a mechanical process of cause and effect. It is more like the multi-faceted, multi-dimensional conversation that God is having with Herself.

Each being is subject to what is called *prarabdha karma*. Prarabdha is that portion of one's total karma that is set to ripen in a particular lifetime. But it may have begun forming in any time and place. So, for instance, the shape of your life is, in part, created from activity set in motion long ago. You also have participated in shaping family, national, human, gender, ethnic and other karmas.

The most important thing to understand is that there is no "bad" or "good" karma. In whatever circumstances you find yourself, you can be certain that you have been given the perfect response to your activity. Every response you receive, no matter how "good" or "bad," contains a wisdom seed with the potential to blossom into greater awakening. Whether or not you recognize that potential and cultivate it is another story.

When we are mostly sleep-walking through our lives, severely limited by our small sense of self, we are unaware of the responsivity of the world to our actions. We cannot hear the world communicating to us. We are compulsive and reactive instead of naturally responsive.

This is very easy to understand in an everyday way. Some people can feel their way gracefully and skillfully through complex situations in life. Other people are always bumping into obstacles because they cannot see the open door.

Our ignorance can function as a kind of innocence. Although we are entangled in cause and effect, our lack of consciousness protects us to some degree. A misbehaving child may be reprimanded, but most people recognize that children are often governed by impulse and cannot be held totally responsible for their actions.

Waking up, we begin to understand more about how Reality functions. We can better sense what is appropriate activity and what is not. We begin to consciously participate in the world conversation, and we are called to a higher level of responsibility for our part. As a result, when we misbehave, the response is more swift and severe.

However, as we continue on the path, we inevitably become attuned to the more subtle nuances of the world communication. So, instead of behaving inappropriately and waking up lifetimes later as we are just beginning to work ourselves out from under some burdensome response, we can notice the response immediately and adjust our activity. Over time, gross corrections become refined. One day, there we are, directly embodying the world's responsiveness. All attachment to correction and karma dissolves in living presence.

At every level, no matter how badly we mess up, the quality of mercy of Self for Self pervades. And mercy reveals itself to us more fully each time we begin to follow our fixations, but then change course and follow wisdom instead.

Through this process, repeated over time, we learn directly that the possibility to surrender our limitations, relax and realize is always present. We get infinite "chances" because every moment is offering us the opportunity to know God. We were never damned, and thus forgiveness is also unnecessary.

We are only guided devotedly by a world Self that is our eternal home, our true Guru and our compassionate Mother, all one and the same: Our Own Self.

FOLLOWING

One night, Ma came to me in a dream and gave me an instruction that I didn't want to follow. I argued with her. She looked into my eyes and wagged her Guru finger at me. She said sternly: *You are shishya (disciple); I am Guru. Your only job is to obey instantly!*

Okay, I answered simply. *Okay,* she replied and smiled at me. My senses and awareness became suffused with bliss and clarity that lasted for days.

When we are just starting out on the path of sadhana, small I is in charge. Small I struggles, asks for help, prays and does mantra and other practices, often in a state of desperation.

More importantly, small I plans, decides, and fights to maintain its false sense of independence. When that is threatened, small I throws tantrums and tries to bargain.

Later, small I relaxes and spreads out a little bit, edging closer to discovering that it is a limited echo of the *Aham* or *I Am* of Lord Shiva. When small I finally lets go, and you are totally immersed in *Aham*, that is moksha (Self-realization).

When we are very tense, we don't communicate well. But when we are more relaxed, we hear more and can respond more appropriately. When we are not so busy defending small I, we start to notice that the world is offering us guidance and assistance.

We can stop struggling and embark on the path of listening and following.

The moment when small I stops aggressively planning, deciding and seeking is a milestone. You are understanding more and more that freedom doesn't mean that small I gets whatever it desires! That would be a terrible outcome because whatever little I desires at this moment is shaped by extreme limitation.

By practicing without pre-determined goals and following your teachers and the wisdom hints given to you as you move through various circumstances, you can discover who you really are, not just who small I thinks you should be.

Many people cannot imagine a life of following. They have some idea that following is weak or dangerous. They cannot envision a life free from worrying about what will happen and free from trying to control life and manage fear.

Inevitably though, following brings deeper relaxation and more moments of simple, spontaneous, skillful responsiveness. By following and taking refuge in wisdom, a deep and abiding confidence in life begins to develop. You come to understand, in a deeply embodied way that the instruction, the giver of instruction, and the follower are one.

A CONVERSATION WITH TIME

Although many of us have forgotten this, the entire manifest world is a time piece. Our mechanical (or digital) watches are a pale reminder of the inexorability of the life process. Stars, planets, seas and our own bodies go *tick tock, tick tock.*

Our bodies converse continuously with natural cycles of living and dying, waxing and waning, creating and destroying, expanding and contracting, revealing and concealing. When we don't live by these natural cycles, our bodies slowly start to forget the correct vocabulary and develop their own, sociopathic language. *I must have caffeine. I can't eat until afternoon. I'll just lie on the couch for another month. I can't sit still. Another beer! Another 80 hour work week!*

Most of the substances Westerners call "medicine" are designed to antidote the ill effects of living out of sync with natural time, or to override natural time with chemical "invincibility."

The energy we expend in trying to step out of natural time is our own.

When we take a medicine that suppresses illness so we can work without resting; when we live at the same breakneck pace, regardless of the season; when we allow our bodies to be anesthetized and cut into for the sake of cosmetic beauty; when we have mechanical sex and remain in depleting friendships, the energy that is being wasted is our own life force. We sink ourselves deeper into energetic debt and move closer to death by exhaustion.

Paradoxically, we strive to look youthful until we die, but we expect to die of disease. When someone dies, our inevitable question is: *What did he or she die of?* We can't imagine a death that is not brought on by decrepitude.

Our view of illness is truly perverse. We live in a soup of chemical pollutants and radiation of various sorts. We take medicines with debilitating side effects as a matter of course. And yet most of us are desperate to avoid illness.

Some spiritually accomplished human beings are able to discern the exact date and time of impending death. They calmly prepare and die in seeming perfect health at the appointed moment. Others have various illnesses, but relate to them quite differently than do less expansive folk.

Anandamayi Ma could see the subtle forms or bodies of illnesses. She related to them with the same compassion she demonstrated toward human beings. She often said, *I don't chase you away. Why should I chase illness away?* If she took medicine, it was only to relieve the anxieties of those around her.

The 16th Karmapa, reincarnate leader of the Buddhist Kagyu tradition, was ravaged by cancer, but he consistently reported that he experienced no pain. Attendants say that throughout his "illness," he never wavered in his concern for those around him. (Elliot, DVD)

For most of us more ordinary practitioners, the rule should be to take care of our bodies in the way that best helps us to work with the karma that will inevitably at times express itself as illness.

This means establishing eating and movement practices that are aligned with your constitution and the seasons. It means becoming knowledgeable about a naturopathic system of daily self-care, such as Ayurveda.

The more expansive your perceptions become through sadhana and healthy everyday self-care, the more subtly you will relate to disease and the process of dying. Healthy or ill, accomplished human beings are supporting their own and others' unfoldment, not working against this natural process.

Anandamayi Ma was often surrounded by people who had grown up in a culture of the denigration of bodies. But she taught that we have no right to misuse our bodies, or care for them improperly.

Listen to your body. Eat when you are hungry. Eat non-toxic foods to the best of your ability. Rest when you are ill or tired. Get a proper amount of sleep consistently. Investigate your constitution by consulting a naturopathic doctor such as an Ayurvedic or Chinese medicine practitioner. Live according to the rhythm of the days and the seasons.

Don't let our stumbling, out of sync culture drag you along with it to chronic depletion and death by exhaustion. This is not the Tantrik way.

For many contemporary people, it is a great adventure to rediscover that our bodies are in a living relationships with the rest of the cosmos, with all of the cosmos. Waking up to one's conversation with time is like regaining your senses a hundred thousand fold. You can start on this great adventure now by taking simple, practical steps in your everyday life.

HEART ADVICE

For everyone, all

KNOWLEDGE = DEVOTION*

WHEN YOU COME to know your Self, you understand that the whole creation is expressing devotion toward itself. You become immersed in the ocean of natural devotion. Everything you do expresses *that*.

Devotion is often associated with the Bhakti movement that swept through India from the 13th to 17th centuries and is still going strong today. The movement arose in response to the exclusionary religious culture of the Brahmin caste. Many people, including lower caste people and women generally, were barred by the Brahmin priest class from participating in ritual and various sadhanas.

The Bhakti movement advocated a direct, unmediated relationship with God through a personal outpouring of love for the divine that could be undertaken by anyone. Bhaktas then and now engage in ritual devotional practices, such as making offerings to one's chosen form of God, and kirtan.

Sometimes people think that one kind of tradition is devotional while another isn't.

The fact is that any path you follow through to the end will lead you to discover devotion because devotion is in the nature of Reality. There is no Self-realization without the discovery of devotion.

Many of the Gurus and siddhas of Tantra in 8th to 12th century Kashmir were highly-educated intellectuals. They engaged with gusto in debates with their peers and wrote about art, drama and philosophy.

They also produced some of the greatest devotional hymns and poetry known to humankind. In fact, I have observed that the more realized one becomes, the more devotional one's writings, practice and mode of teaching becomes.

Devotion is everyone's practice in the end because it is God's practice. And realization means realizing one has always been God.

To know oneself is to know the heart of devotion.

It is also to solve the riddle of God's existence.

What makes God divine is not the omnipotence of God. Power is simply power. Being everywhere is simply being everywhere. Immortality is just immortality.

What makes divinity divine is God's uninterrupted, unconditioned, spontaneous clarity, awareness, delight, creativity and devotion. *This is what God, or Reality, is, and we feel about God the same way God feels about everything.* Solved.

* Thanks to Sada'Saya Dyczkowski for this formulation.

WALK SLOWLY AND REMEMBER

What is required of a pilgrim on the Supreme Path is that he should ever keep on walking. To spend one's time in the remembrance of the Eternal does indeed mean to be a traveller on this Path. —Anandamayi Ma (*Ananda Varta* 4.1: 59)

Students often want to know how to fit spiritual practice into their busy lives. Even if a practice only takes ten or twenty minutes, sometimes people can't decide to do it.

Instead, they may spend years struggling with themselves about doing, or not doing. This takes much more energy and time than just sitting for some few minutes! But at least they are thinking about the world with a bit of a larger View. This is a painful way to progress, but it really is better than nothing.

The only reason we don't go along more easily with the natural process of waking up is because we get distracted by the momentum of our karmic habit patterns.

When students ask teachers for advice about how to "fit" spiritual practice into their day, or if they insist that they cannot practice because of other obligations, generally people want strategies for squeezing more into an already overcrowded life.

A student of mine who didn't manage to settle into a regular practice after coming to teachings for a couple of years continually invoked the mantra that he only wanted to "add and not subtract." He was an over-worker and an over-player, but he didn't want to give anything up to make room for spiritual practice. This caused him unhappiness, but he wasn't ready to make a change.

The answer to this kind of karmic dilemma is to just to wait until your longing for Self-discovery grows stronger. You will eventually reach a tipping point where that longing begins to shift the momentum in your life toward making room for activities that help you to wake up.

This is fine, but if you are able to do some practice every day, you can discover much faster.

I try to impress on my students that all I do is walk, day by day, putting one foot in front of the other. I just keep practicing. Every day. In this way, any ordinary person such as myself discovers an extraordinary world.

Doing practice of some kind, and remembering God, or Guru or your real destination every day is the most important, life-changing thing you can do.

When you practice every day, even if it is only for twenty minutes, you begin to remember. You begin to remember who you are. You begin to wake up from the slumber we call normal life.

You will discover more fruit if you practice at the same time every day, and if you remember to be in the state of your practice at other times while you are going about your daily activities. You can do this by recalling how you felt when you were done the practice, and by thinking of your teacher, or God or of your longing for home. You should try to remember and cultivate longing.

This is how to practice when you have a full life, but you are ready to let your longing lead you. Over time, longing will grow. Eventually it will become a river of longing that takes you home.

YOUR FIRST DARK NIGHT OF THE SOUL

Back in the 16th century, the Christian mystic St. John of the Cross wrote about the dark night of the soul. He captured for every age thereafter the essence of an *arid and dark night of contemplation* during which spiritual seekers are inevitably confronted with the reality of their own limitations (67).

The first dark night of the soul generally occurs for sincere practitioners when the blush of initial enthusiasm for the spiritual path begins to give way to the recognition of the reality of our bondage to our compulsive patterns of body, energy and mind.

We begin to recognize the habits we have enjoyed for what they are: purposeful distractions from our fundamental anxiety about our existence.

During this first dark night, we recognize the people we criticize or denigrate as mirrors of our own feelings of lack, worthlessness and self-hatred. Where small I has always comfortably sought meaning and refuge, we find a deep, dark void.

Our lives seem to have fallen into a crevice. We try to scramble back to the comforts and hiding places that have always served us. We quickly find that we have lost the ability to fool ourselves that the pursuit of worldly success, food, friends, sex, pleasure or the latest techno gadget is going to rid us of loneliness and anxiety.

Yet, we are nearly beginners on the path, and so we also doubt the way forward.

We don't know which way to turn; no way seems like the right way. We no longer feel we have a stable identity, or a secure place in the world. We experience grief and fear.

This is a supreme moment of choice for any person. When we fall into 'gaps' where old ways cannot be resurrected and new ways have not yet solidified, we have an opportunity to discover our real motivation, our real longing, and to take responsibility for that, affirm it and act on it.

This first dark night of the soul is the time to stop fighting, fixing, running from or identifying with our fear and sadness. It is a time to sit quietly and allow obsolete self-concepts to fall away.

Then, in contemplation in the space of the heart, we rediscover the diamond-like natural longing for Reality, for God, that is our true inheritance, our royal road to wisdom. It is time to rediscover the indestructible wisdom that got us onto the path in the first place.

When we do discover that wisdom, affirm it, cultivate it and grasp it as our one and only guide, all questions of purpose, meaning and direction will end. We will have discovered that the life process itself is about waking up.

This initial dark night of the soul is also the time to cry out, to reach out and ask for nourishment from our teachers and our communities. It is the time to gather whatever confidence you have in life, and turn decisively toward life, even in the midst of despair.

If the dark night of the soul is traversed with courage and supreme softness, with responsibility and surrender, on the other side is a new confidence in life, a new awareness of how the life process is always moving us toward greater Self-revelation. We can discover the loving responsiveness of life to our sincere efforts.

SPIRITUAL RETREATS

Spiritual retreats are not just for monks and hard-core yogis, and they don't have to last for years.

Direct realization traditions, such as Kashmir Shaivism and Dzogchen, are largely populated by householders—by people living in the work-a-day world with families and other responsibilities. If you are a householder and go on a retreat for several years, you may have no house to hold when you get back!

The key to a retreat is that, for some period of time, you devote yourself 100 percent to sadhana and to relaxing more deeply. Even when you cook, take walks and lounge around during a retreat, it is always within the context of deepening your awareness of Reality. You are doing these things in an undistracted way to the best of your ability. When you become distracted, you are able to notice this more easily than if your condition were masked by the general distraction we call normal life.

In retreat, we get to taste our practice more deeply, develop greater awareness of the essence state. We are more nakedly confronted with our actual condition as the noise of our usual lives subsides.

Good times to go on retreat are when:

> ✤ you receive a new practice from your teacher and want to bond with it;
>
> ✤ you feel the need for rejuvenating and reconnecting with your spiritual life;
>
> ✤ you are genuinely curious about retreats and are ready to explore a deeper commitment to practice;
>
> ✤ you have encountered some blockage in your sadhana, and your teacher recommends a retreat; or
>
> ✤ you enter a particularly good time astrologically for a retreat and want to take advantage of this.

More advanced students may be asked by their teachers to go on regular retreats, and some practitioners continue to undertake retreats throughout their lives.

The prospect of even a very short retreat can bring up longing, excitement and fear. The busyness and business of life help us to avoid taking responsibility for our loneliness, anxiety, anger, exhaustion and lack of fulfillment. In retreat, such avoidance is more difficult. So we feel a little fear about that. But if it is the right time for you to go on retreat, you will also sense the opportunity to relax and take refuge in your real nature more deeply.

Anandamayi Ma organized week-long retreats during which householders could enjoy and encounter a short amount of time dedicated 100 percent to spiritual practice. The week encompassed diet, daily routine, satsang, kirtan and meditation. Although these retreats were quite rigorous for your average householder, people loved them so much, the events continue to this day.

Ma also used to require regular periods of *mauna* (silence) for those living in her ashrams. This is also a kind of retreat.

A properly organized retreat can help us to directly recognize what it is we really are longing for in this life and to find the means and the courage to embrace that more fully. In the process, we enhance our capacity to relax and receive real nourishment.

A successful retreat for those in a beginning or intermediate stage of practice will proceed with a definite plan. You should know beforehand what practices you are going to do, and you should factor in time for just living and getting more in tune with nature. You should ask your teacher for advice about what to do if you run into roadblocks.

A retreat can last for a half-day, a day, a few days or longer. Having a definite plan and guidance from a teacher allows you to relax more and derive more benefit from your time alone.

When I was in my early twenties, I went on a three-day retreat in upstate New York in the middle of winter. The retreat was in a very small hut—not big enough to stand up in—on the side of a snow-covered mountain. A kerosene stove provided the only heat. People from the group who owned the land brought food twice a day and left it outside.

I had received no spiritual instruction at all, had never practiced and had no idea what to do on a retreat. Frankly, I don't even know where I got the idea. In addition, the kerosene stove gave off fumes. So I spent the time in a stupor of sleepiness and anxiety. This is what you should *not* do!

If you already have a teacher and feel a desire to experience retreat, you can ask your teacher for help structuring your time. If you have been instructed in some kind of mantra or meditation or ritual, you can take useful retreat days even if you don't have a regular teacher.

In this case, you can ask a more experienced friend how to structure a retreat. Or you can contact a local center in the tradition to which you feel most connected and ask for advice from a teacher there. Perhaps you have been going to classes or meditations. Don't be afraid to ask.

A retreat is not about doing constant seated practice. While there will be definite practices to do, you should always remember to take spiritual refreshment. Movement and taking time to reconnect with nature should be a regular aspect of your day.

A good way to orient yourself to simple spiritual refreshment is to consider that refreshment means both rest and nourishment.

Spiritual refreshment is not work. It is not exercise. And it is not self-improvement. When you sit to meditate, walk in nature, breath in good air, gaze at the sky, enjoy uncontrived life or read or listen to spiritual teachings, you are receiving real food. You can relax and relish this subtle food just as if you were eating a sumptuous meal or drinking in the most delicious elixir. Eventually, refreshment will become your moment-to-moment experience.

KINDNESS AND ANCESTRAL KARMA

Ancestors are people to whom we are immediately, biologically related and who have died. Traditionally, when we work with our ancestors in a conscious way through ritual and prayer, we are including seven generations of ancestors. As spiritual practitioners, we also consciously relate to the Gurus from past lives who are our spiritual ancestors.

The real-time presence of ancestors is a fact of life for millions of people all over the world. Here in the West, many of us aren't really sure who our ancestors are, or why they are important. We may remember a grandparent or an aunt with great fondness, or with more conflicted emotions. We may, if we are a little more open, feel the presence of a deceased relative or two. But we generally have a hard time connecting with the living reality of our continuity in time with our ancestors.

In order to better understand and develop a beneficial relationship to our ancestors, we should remember the three gates of human life: body, energy and mind. These are the fundamental ways that consciousness (Shiva) and primordial Shakti show up in a human being.

Body, energy body, and our minds are all conditioned. This means we are having an experience of limitation. Our bodies, energy bodies and minds have individualized styles. The beauty of the world is that, through investigating and working with our limitations expressed through the three gates, we have the possibility to discover Reality in its fullness and embody that. This is the process of Self-realization.

In one, absolutely literal sense, our ancestors are living *as* us. They contributed in a concrete way to how our bodies, energy and minds are showing up in this moment.

A common way of talking about this is by invoking genetics. Our genes are produced by karmic forces and are a gross embodiment of karma. For people who cannot understand or work directly with karma, genes provide a more tangible, yet potentially less profoundly transformative, alternative.

Karma is more subtle than genetics. We are all composed of karma, of patterned consciousness and energy. The patterns that expressed our ancestors do not go away just because their physical bodies have dissolved. The strongest patterns, the strongest karmas, are living simultaneously with us in time.

Say, for instance, you have an ancestor composed of the usual collection of human expressions—some "problems" and some capacities. But if this ancestor's signal characteristic was exceptional kindness, then the pattern of kindness will persist and be beneficial to you. You can be concretely helped by this in your present life. That pattern is still alive, and so you and your ancestor are living simultaneously in the present.

On the other hand, we all have some patterns we are related to that are stuck in compulsion mode: compulsive anger, grief, excessive hunger and so on. These are also very strong patterns. We can feel them in our three gates, and sometimes we can sense these influences in other ways.

It is important not to feel afraid or to demonize our ancestors. They are just another aspect of our total karma. They are ourselves. As a practitioner, you have a special responsibility to help your ancestors by treating yourself, them, and others with kindness.

Kindness is the universal medicine that will free you and your ancestors from their fixations.

This is the key. You and your ancestral patterns are one package in time. By freeing yourself, you also relax those karmas for your entire ancestral line. Every time you relax and are able to express kindness toward yourself, your ancestors and others, you create greater freedom for all. In this way, by doing your practice and discovering real kindness, pernicious influences become helpful influences.

Having come in contact with the teachings, having established a practice, and now understanding more about your ancestors, it is actually your responsibility to assist by developing your own capacity to express spontaneous kindness.

In terms of our immediate families, whatever family you have been born into, you can count on the fact that something in this total situation is expressive of your karma and also gives you the opportunity, however painful, to move in the direction of relaxing that karma. Whether or not you choose to do that in this lifetime is another question.

Working with our family karma does not necessarily mean being in literal contact with our birth families. There are infinite ways and means. However it does mean recognizing the fundamental fact of the communicativeness of all life. That we are born into a certain family is a communication. We must learn to listen to and respond appropriately to that.

THE HABIT OF SELF-REALIZATION

People often ask: *Do I have to practice every day?* Or more commonly: *Do I have to practice at the same time every day?*

During her lifetime, Anandamayi Ma, spoke to tens of thousands of householders—people living busy lives with families and jobs. Most of the people to whom she spoke had no intention of becoming yogis or yoginis.

Ma's exhortation was always the same: Set aside a small amount of time each day—just ten or fifteen minutes at the same hour–for repeating one of the names of God (mantra *japa*).

Mantras anyone can chant are OM Mā, or OM Namo Nārāyani, or OM Namah Shivāya.

Ma said:

> *Karma accumulated for ages and ages is wiped out by God's sacred Name. Just as lighting a lamp illumines a cave that has been in darkness for centuries, even so the obscurity of numberless births is annihilated by the power of a divine name. (Matri Vani II 193)*

The momentum of our habits is strong. We are, as they say, creatures of habit. Habit is the overwhelming flavor of our lives. We suffer from habitual emotions, thoughts and activities.

The Tantras teach us that we rise by that which we fall.

We are "good" at habitual behavior and, for this reason, forming habits is a capacity that we can employ to relax and refine our energy. If we establish even a small new habit in the direction of Self-realization, we are eventually victorious in conquering karma.

Why is this?

Because a habit of Self-realization *always* has more power than habits of ignorance. In the end, freedom always trumps enslavement. This is a law of Reality, verified by yogis throughout time. The names of God and Guru given to us for japa are clear, sweet water dripping on rock; they eventually break down the rock into sand and our tensions flow away.

However, if the water drips only intermittently, the transformation will not take place.

Ten or fifteen minutes of japa, or other spiritual practice, done each day at the same time, consistently throughout one's life, will have a large effect, much more than stopping and starting, or sporadic yoga classes or workshops.

Anyone can resolve to do this. You don't need a Guru or any money. And you don't need to take my word for it. You can try it yourself and find out.

THE PURPOSE OF LIFE

The sole purpose of human life is to Self-realize. When we do practice, after a time we discover that this purpose was built-in all along. In fact, waking up is so ingrained in Reality, it's hardly correct to call that a "purpose." It's just Nature accomplishing itself.

You don't need, and shouldn't seek, any other justification for your life.

This doesn't mean that we should drop everything and head for remote mountain caves. We must eat and take basic care of ourselves and our dependents. We are, most of us, engaged in some kind of necessary work.

All of these aspects of our lives are also Shiva nature. We can discover our enlightened Self in any situation if we do not allow ourselves to get too distracted by karmic emotions and ambition.

Find something to do that makes a positive contribution, that you enjoy and that leaves you enough energy to keep doing your practice and participating in non-work aspects of life. Try not to over-identify with what you do to earn money. Your job is to Self-realize. You've had that job since you were conceived, and you'll never be laid off!

Carry out your responsibilities very simply — just like you brush your teeth in the morning and night. Don't make a big deal out of life's duties. Appreciate their rhythms and try not to over do.

Make daily practice and remembering your true nature your main "business." Integrate practices such as mantra and guru yoga into your everyday activities. Try to remain undistracted from the inner orientation that urges you onward toward Self-recognition.

The best way to approach the householder life is to keep remembering that by making efforts to wake up, you are already going along with the life process. You have already found the purpose of your life. You can relax.

IS NONATTACHMENT BORING?

This question comes from a student who is practicing every day without fail. The same question asked by a non-practitioner would, perhaps, receive a different answer.

Nonattachment is often misunderstood. It does not refer to a condition of emotional blandness, coldness or lack of caring. Neither is it an affected stance of nonchalance.

Nonattachment means you are fine with whatever happens.

Maybe you already understand that life has ups and downs, and this is normal and fine. There is nothing to rail against. Sometimes you will work hard and not get the desired outcome. Sometimes people will do things that you experience as hurtful. You will inevitably fall ill.

In the midst of these occurrences, you may feel disappointed or sad, but you are not outraged. You do not feel victimized by the simple fact that unpleasant things happen. Approaching life in this way is an expression of ordinary nonattachment.

On a more expansive level, nonattachment means you have embodied the understanding that all outcomes and circumstances are equal.

All actors, all situations and all outcomes are Shiva nature. Shiva is the player, the played, the object of play and the result. Every outcome is equal because only one, continuous consciousness is enacting all of this.

For instance, a person acting in a soap opera does not feel that a scene of betrayal is better than a scene of a wedding. These are common occurrences in soap operas! The actor or actress knows that they are equally scenes in a drama.

Just so, Shiva nature is enacting every possible form and experience of manifest life. From the perspective of Shiva nature, or a highly realized person, all scenes participate in this equality.

At this level of identifying with one's real nature, there is a spontaneous and relaxed display of emotions, including sadness and anger. There is no blandness. All emotions are also Shiva nature. There is simply no feeling that anything needs to be controlled or defended against.

Emotions arise and subside naturally and appropriately. They don't stick around and become habit patterns. Whatever is displayed by such persons, their condition is the same. They are always aware of their essence nature and of expressing that.

Furthermore, for more realized people, kindness, compassion and devotion flow never-endingly in many forms. There is not one hint of coldness unless it is a display for someone's benefit. Nor is there any concept of "being compassionate" or "cultivating compassion." The wisdom virtues of compassion and devotion manifest with total spontaneity as these virtues are what composes Reality itself.

The most highly realized human beings—the avatars or direct emanations of God—are always full of laughter, sweetness and playfulness.

Ordinary habitual, emotional reaction patterns, on the other hand, are effortfully whipped-up dramas. They are dramas in which the actors have forgotten they are acting! They arise from a nearly constant state of hysterical attachment to pleasure and an aversion to pain.

You want this. You don't want that. You are afraid to lose people, places, things and arrangements. You live in a push-pull frenzy, trying to control what comes, what goes, what stays and what never arrives. This approach to life is fundamentally fearful and manipulative.

When we begin to do regular spiritual practice, our conduct and energy begin to recalibrate. We come more into tune with the natural state. The feeling of neutrality, or even numbness, arises in contrast to our fading hysteria.

Boredom is a unique expression of this process. All along, we had been cultivating an artificial feeling of aliveness with all of our exaggerated emotions and reactions. When we begin to relax that effort, we first feel tired and perhaps a bit bland. Then we begin to notice the real quality of our energy when we aren't doing anything to manipulate it or project it forcefully outward.

Boredom is actually an energetically dynamic situation. Think of the feeling of boredom. It has an uncomfortable vibratory quality.

When you are in the process of recovering your natural relationship to your Shakti, you can feel as if you are crawling with energy. Or you may feel that you don't know what to do with your energy. You are bursting to do something, but your usual outlets are no longer so appealing. Shakti that you had been wastefully pouring out is returning to its proper place. Some people call these intermediate states "boredom."

If you keep going, you will begin to notice a beautiful quality of spaciousness and relaxation. You begin to experience a relaxed liveliness. There is no more need for drama. Yet, you no longer feel numb. You come home to natural enjoyment.

KEEP THE VIEW AS YOUR CONSTANT FRIEND

Imagine ant theologians trying to explain the "contradiction" that God provides enormous feasts, but so many ant-kind die trying to enjoy the bounty (e.g. so many ants get sprayed when they invade someone's food cabinet, or get smashed at human picnics!).

Contradictions arise when you try to understand a different mode of experiencing from your more limited perspective. All contradictions prove, in the end, to be phantasms arising from limited View.

In some spiritual traditions, students are at first taught only "relative View." So you are taught that you have problems and you should try to improve, or even chastise yourself. Later, if at all, you might be taught that everything is fine.

In the tradition of direct realization Tantra, students receive the entire View all at once. There is not so much of a distinction between relative and absolute View. In fact, we go one step further and acknowledge that the ultimate teaching is to hold no View. "Being Shiva" means just relaxing in unconditioned *samavesha*, or immersion, wide awake, enjoying our own nature: flowing presence.

Until then, we keep the View as our constant friend, even in the midst of experiences of limitation. We work with our current condition of limitation while holding in our awareness the understanding that our real nature is unlimited. It is a kind of juggling act, but Tantrikas enjoy juggling!

In this way, we can develop the capacity to dis-identify with our "problems," even while we have to acknowledge and work with our feeling that life is problematic. Got that? ☺

The Sanskrit word for View is *darshan*. View is to see without limitation, to see the whole picture, the largest context, to see our original face, our essential nature. View is also the instruments through which we see: our teachers, community, sadhana, and scripture.

View is the most important thing a teacher can transmit to a student. When we are infused with the correct View, we always have a guide to reorient us in our seated practice and daily life. When I know my true context, when I am taught the correct use of those instruments through which to see, when I have seen my true face, then, no matter what happens, no matter what "mistakes" I may make, I always have a reminder, a sign post, a way home. Of course, having View, one must also find the courage to remember it and live it.

At one level of experiencing, we are subject to karmic tensions. We are having a real experience of limitation, and we suffer. We do spiritual practice to transform our experience.

We always have to work honestly from the base of our actual experience, not from where we wish we were. Otherwise, our practice has no authenticity or appropriateness and will not bear fruit.

At the level of awareness unconditioned by karma, the idea that there could be a problem, or a contradiction makes no sense. Everything that arises, everything that happens or doesn't happen, is the free expression of Shiva nature, of consciousness and energy. Every free expression of Shiva nature, including the experience of having problems, is equal and fine. So the experience of having problems is also no problem.

The student does sadhana and works with her tensions. At the same time, through transmission, she is cultivating a real connection to a more subtle and expansive mode of awareness. Even in times of extreme limitation, she tries to remember and connect.

All of our practices, even the most beginning practices, are done this way.

TANTRA FRESH AND ORIGINAL

One Thanksgiving eve, I dreamt that some old friends (aka old habits) were making a Thanksgiving feast, but I wasn't invited. Right in the middle of this dream, I began to experience intense pain in my chest and an intense feeling of grief. I was aware in the dream of the karmic nature of this pain. Even while feeling this pain to the maximum, I also had some perspective on it.

Doing sadhana enables one to have this kind of perspective, even in the midst of reactivity. So, at some point, I took a strong decision. I decided to leave the house of pain and go outside to explore.

Outside, everything was shimmering with fresh, vibrant life.

I saw lakes and mountains and trails. Small birds and other animals frolicked in grass sparkling with new rain. People's faces were also eloquently expressive. At some point, I came upon a green, rolling park filled with diverse, beautiful animals, and a tiger was running, its stripes flashing out from between the trees.

I had no particular place to go and no expectations. I was just exploring and enjoying. Everything that occurred was full of interest, intelligence and immediacy.

There is freshness and originality to the situation of being alive and being aware in life. In order to experience this freshness and originality, we have to step out of karma. Karma means habit patterns — good or bad.

Frankly, though, most of us are firmly convinced that our habits are who we are. So we don't want to step out of them. From our limited perspective, stepping out of habit feels like dying. And it is a dying. As Tantrikas, having the courage to let old forms of life die is absolutely necessary. We have to cultivate this courage and revise our View of death.

When habit patterns are getting ready to die, they make a last stand. They become more intense. They feel all-encompassing as if we will never be able to escape from them.

Part of maturing as a practitioner is being able to discern when this process of dying is occurring, and to just keep going on with our practice, day-by-day. In due time, the pattern will pop and naturally dissolve.

The way to boldly step out of karma is not necessarily to attack your habit patterns, or try to aggressively rout them out. Anandamayi Ma taught that there is no need to renounce anything. Everything that needs to fall away will fall away naturally under the gentle force of our sadhana. Be bold and just keep practicing no matter what. In this way, you can trade in your limited knowing and conceptualizing for real experiencing and a direct encounter with originality and freshness.

AHIMSA

Ahimsa, or nonviolence, is often interpreted as "not killing" or "not hurting" others. But how can we possibly avoid hurting others when we are busy harming ourselves? In fact, how can we avoid harming others when we are not even aware of the myriad ways in which we harm ourselves at every moment?

Tantra teaches us that establishing ourselves with awareness in the natural state is the foundation upon which we can live a life of ahimsa or nonharming. We must tend to our own liberation first before we can entertain the idea that we know what is good for others.

There is no way around this. Congratulating ourselves that our conduct toward others is exemplary when we are still caught up in the many tensions of self-harm only reinforces those tensions and sinks us deeper and deeper into unawareness.

The original "harm" is our fervent conviction that we are separate from others, that we possess an "I" distinct from all else that is. This small I insists on defending its feeling of having boundaries, and this insistence drives the compulsions and habits we call normal life.

All of our defensive, repetitive thoughts and behaviors are geared toward reinforcing small I. The more we relax through the process of sadhana and open to grace, the more these patterns of compulsion stand out in relief, and the more we notice how they control every moment of our lives.

Without this awareness, painful as it may be, we are living in a fog through which both ourselves and others are only dimly visible. The larger context of our lives is obscured.

But we are not helpless. We can refrain from gross harms against ourselves and others by following the precepts laid out for us by our teachers and traditions. Slowly, the compulsion called small I relaxes and the world rushes in to greet us, along with true understanding.

The primordial ahimsa is self-love expressed as a sincere commitment to gaining freedom from our compulsive experience of separation.

Sitting across a table from a friend of mine in Varanasi, I said: *Isn't it beautiful that this world allows us to look into each others' eyes and experience ourselves as two!*

The capacity for dualistic experience is a precious gift, but only if it is an expression of playfulness, and not a prison of compulsion.

Individuals do not exist, but individual experiencing emerges and subsides within the context of the entire field of experiencing. When we realize this process through sadhana, there is no longer any compulsion to defend small I or "my experience."

This is the beginning of true ahimsa.

YOU CAN ALWAYS SERVE

No matter in what condition you find yourself, you can always serve. No matter how low you feel about yourself, even if your life is falling apart, you can always contribute something positive by serving others.

For this reason, service is the great refuge.

I can say: *Take refuge in your own nature.* You might feel that you don't have this capacity. But you don't have to be highly realized to take refuge in service. What a wonderful circumstance!

People have various feelings about seva (service to teacher and community) and karma yoga. When I was much younger, I used to call seva, "slave-a."

Now, I am so happy to be able to serve in any moment, in every moment. There is no need to fight with myself, or tackle complicated "problems." I don't have to worry about anything, or try to accomplish anything difficult. I can just serve.

You can cook a meal. Wash a window. Weed a garden. Lend a hand with shopping. Clean something. Dust off altars. Teach someone. Run an errand. Practice any old small kindness, including offering a kind word, or kindly listening. In any moment, in every moment, you can offer service to your teacher, to your teacher's family, to your community, to your friends, or to a stranger.

When you are taking refuge in service, you feel really grateful to be able to do just that. Serving with gratitude for being at least able to serve, despite all of one's other limitations, is the *mahabhava* (great attitude) of all real service.

Sometimes you hear people talk about "selfless service." They mean serving without any attachment to getting something in return, including admiration from others. Taking refuge in service is a somewhat different orientation to serving.

Taking refuge in service, you realize that we are all in the same boat. You need refuge from all of your inner and outer machinations. When you are serving, you can just focus on that activity and feel satisfied with yourself.

Others also need support. When you are satisfied—feeling your simple, essential goodness as you serve—that feeling is automatically shared with others.

By serving, everyone feels, at least a bit, that samsara is okay. Life is not so much of a burden. We can express simple care about ourselves and each other by performing these little acts. What a relief!

The best aspect of service is that, with these simple acts, you actually *are* taking refuge in your own nature. The fundamental nature of God is devotional. The dance of service is God's dance. Your own Self. In every moment.

SHORT PATH, LONG PATH

One night, I dreamt of a house. I was leading students outside into a vast, rolling landscape of shimmering color.

I said to them, *How beautiful! How infinitely nuanced! How luminous! Please, please come.*

Some stepped directly from the confines of the familiar house into the outdoors. Others were afraid and hung back. I wanted to wait for everyone.

When students meet the right teachings for them, a vast, subtle landscape opens out. Longing to explore that arises. There is recognition and a feeling of discovering one's true, unconfined home. This is a gap in karma, a gap in time.

But often, immediately following this gap experience, fear rushes in. Each person's fear of waking up takes a familiar karmic form.

What if I change too much and lose friends?

What if my spiritual practice interferes with my career?

What if my family freaks out?

I don't want to lose anything; I only want to add things.

I don't like to be in a group.

I don't like to feel uncomfortable; I only want to feel happy.

I don't like being asked to pay for teachings.

I don't need a teacher.

Teacher is not behaving as I want.

I wanted spiritual practice to be X and the teacher is asking me to do Y.

I'm confused.

I'm not capable.

This isn't the right time.

I'm too busy.

I don't want to travel for teachings.

I'm angry.

I just want to know how to fix my problems.

I have to understand everything thoroughly before I get started.

The culture of these teachings is strange to me.

I need the teacher, or my practice, to be miraculous; nothing less will convince me to continue.

I can't sit still.

I think too much.

I'm tired.

I don't want to practice.

I don't want to practice.

I don't want to practice.

My teacher, Anandamayi Ma, manifested infinite patience. At the same time, she did everything possible to help people to recognize their real natures. She both waited for students to be able to practice, and, at the same time, tried to give them everything they needed to make that happen quickly.

If you want to release your resistance and Self-realize a little more quickly, you must put yourself in situations that remind you of who you are, of your true home. You must make an effort to overcome the karmic momentum that takes the form of stories about why you can't, don't want to, or shouldn't do this.

Read the works of teachers you admire and biographies and auto-biographies of practitioners. Attend teachings whenever possible. If you have a teacher, seize every opportunity to receive teachings from that person. If you have been given a practice, do it with consistency and constancy as if your life depends on it—because it does.

Try to remember that, although most of us will lead an ordinary life with ordinary responsibilities, the purpose of this entire manifestation is Self-realization.

Anything that you claim is standing in your way, no matter how reasonable-sounding, is only karmic vision. There is no reasonable reason not to step out of your limitations, other than the workings of limitation itself.

Time and karma are intimately related. Ma knew that everything has its time, and that it is also possible to step out of linear time.

So, on the one hand, it is perfectly fine that students take a long time to dedicate themselves consciously to Self-realization, that they are continually coming and going. Every reason students give not to practice, every little bit of resistance is just the life process itself unfolding in time.

This is what Ma called "the long way." We live through every bit of karma until it fully ripens and falls away.

If we try to directly realize our true nature, this is what Ma called "the short way." We recognize the transmission of Self-realization coming through our teachers, and we work directly to embody that in every moment. We have the opportunity to sidestep the full impact of our karma and enter directly into the unconditioned, eternal moment.

MA IS PRESENT

A certain Swami Nirgunananda served as Anandamayi Ma's secretary for the last three years of her life. I met him, and he shared with me a phrase in Bengali commonly uttered by Ma:

Mā āchen. Kiser chintā?

As Swamiji translated it for me, it means: Ma is here. Why worry?

When a mother rushes to comfort a small child, usually says: *I am here. Everything is fine now.*

As adults, we receive the news that "I am here," for instance, when a friend is comforting us in a time of need, as an indication that we can relax. We are not alone. Someone else has come to our rescue. The world may be big and bad, but we have a friend.

But Anandamayi Ma says: *I am here. I am present. Why worry?*

I am there, in your troubles, too. There is nothing but the Supreme I.

I am present in everything, as everything. There is nothing but the Supreme I.

If every happening is nothing other than I, why worry?

The Supreme Intelligence is All. I am your body, your life, your troubles and your sadhana. You are never alone or apart.

These are not concepts. The presence of the Supreme Self can be experienced directly by anyone who is constant in doing sadhana. This presence, which is presence itself, can be felt, seen, understood and lived.

At the same time, I am also this body and you are that body. This is one way of experiencing the Supreme Self. And this is the everyday experience of most human beings.

And so, Ma comes, in the form of Guru, in the form of a human mother, in the form of a friend. She plays the game of duality for her own delight and out of compassion for those who as of yet know nothing else.

She manifests here in an ordinary way, for us.

When Anandamayi Ma was asked: *Why are you here?* She would answer in the voice of the Supreme Self: *Because you called me.*

Self calls to Self and always answers in the appropriate form. When we call out for Mother or Guru, she inevitably arrives.

Worrying is one of the main "tools" we use to try to grab on and stop the flow of life. When we "worry" about something, we grab onto it and won't let go. Worries live in our mind, filling up the void that we wish to avoid. It doesn't matter what we are worrying about: simply to engage in the distracting, controlling activity of worrying is why we worry.

It is possible to live in the world, troubles and all, without worry, without continuously holding on, if we remember Ma is here. She is the ocean of consciousness and compassion. We can relax and take refuge in Her.

BARDO

Do you start to wail and cry if a person goes to another room in the house? This death is inevitably connected with this life. In the sphere of Immortality, where is the question of death and loss? Nobody is lost to me.
—Sri Anandamayi Ma (qted. in Mukerji, "Sri Ma Anandamayi")

MESSAGES FROM ANOTHER ROOM

I CAN BARELY remember Dayavati before she got cancer. I think she may have started e-mailing me in response to postings here at Jaya Kula. She was born in Jamaica, but had lived in Toronto for many years.

In any case, we have the same diksha Guru. She had been initiated many years before I was. I knew of her for quite some time before we became close. It happened that during the last several years of her life, while she was ill, we spoke weekly or even more frequently.

Dayavati had triple negative cancer, a drug-resistant cancer that is more prevalent in people of African descent. Most of our conversations were about spiritual practice and, in the last six months or so, about dying as a practitioner.

Like the rest of us, Dayavati's strengths both helped her and got her into trouble. And her troubles often led her back to herself and her practice.

She was courageous and stubborn. Persevering and fearful. Big-hearted and demanding. Vibrant, vivacious and ruefully attached to food that was not helpful to her.

Dayavati was a practitioner, above all. Not the kind you read about in books, but the kind most people are: chipping away at fears and fixations day-by-day. Zooming ahead, waffling, taking detours, running around in circles, finding her ground, making excuses, courageously facing the truth and then forgetting it again until next time.

Dayavati loved her teachers, and she loved Ma. Even though she buckled down to daily practice only in the last two years of her life, she truly understood and embodied devotion. She had a spectacular, unwavering devoted heart.

The cancer, however, was aggressive and wily: a karmic, and likely ancestral juggernaut.

After many surgeries, rounds of radiation and chemo, visits to expert acupuncturists, naturopaths, and healers, the cancer had appeared in both breasts and taken one of them, fractured her spine, and invaded her liver, lungs and brain.

Dayavati passed into the bardos on Monday, December 1, 2008. She was surrounded by friends, sangha and family. She was fifty-two years old.

The last time I spoke to Dayavati, she could no longer move, eat or drink. Edema had crept into her abdomen. Breath was decreasing. She spoke only an occasional single word.

She was withdrawing, preserving whatever strength she had for the transition.

Her sister kindly held the phone to Dayavati's ear. I told Dayavati that her entire spiritual community worldwide was holding her in their hearts and practicing for her.

In a voice so depleted of prana, I could barely make out her words, she said: "I feel it. Thank you."

I spoke a few other words, mainly encouraging her to relax. And then I reminded her that she could do Guru yoga, and I repeated Om Ma several times. This was a mantra Dayavati loved.

She then began saying, over and over again in a more distinct voice: I remember, I remember, I remember.

There was a note of childlike wonder, even happiness, as if she had indeed forgotten and was glad to rediscover something so familiar and fundamental.

Every practitioner works to remember the habit of practice during the transits of death and the bardos. I felt reassured and deeply moved.

In the way that she lived and died, Dayavati left us with many profound messages to reflect upon.

The first message is this. No matter how, as practitioners, we struggle to stay on the path, no matter what our so-called failings or lapses—and we all experience these in abundance—keeping on, until the time of death, remembering, remembering, remembering and remembering again is a great victory. A great, great victory.

So, Jai Jai Jai Dayavati Sarasvati!

You will never be lost.

OM AIM GUM SHRI GURUBHYO NAMAH

OM SHRI MATRE NAMAH

OM MATA ANANDAMAYI SVAHA

GLOSSARY OF SANSKRIT WORDS

Abhisheka — blessing bath; initiation; anointing

Ahimsa — nonviolence

Asana — literally, "seat"; a yoga posture

Anavamala — the root limitation; ignorance of one's own nature; the experience of being separate

Bhakti — a personal, intense and loving attachment to a form of God; a spiritual path utilizing disciplined, intense feelings of love and devotion for God

Bhava — feeling-orientation; disposition; a spiritual mood

Bhedabheda — dual-nondual

Chakra — one of the subtle structures that comprises the energy body; "wheel"

Crore — ten million

Darshan — sight; gaze; outlook; stance or View

Diksha — initiation

Dinacharya — Ayurvedic practice of daily ritual; literally "daily conduct"

Eka rasa — one taste

Guru — heavy; remover of darkness; an accomplished spiritual teacher

Guru tattva — the Guru element; the Guru function of Reality

Ishta devata — tutelary deity; one's chosen deity

Japa — the practice of repeating a mantra

Kali Yuga — the age of ignorance lasting 432,000 years

Karma —activity conditioned by cause and effect; conditioned, repeating patterns of consciousness and energy

Karma yoga: selfless service

Kriya — spontaneous, unconditioned activity

Kriya yoga — largely internal yoga utilizing the subtle energy body, breath and awareness

Kula — spiritual family; group of initiates of a Guru

Lila — the play or sport of the Supreme Self

Loka — realm, or world

Madhyama — Shakti manifesting as silent mental articulation

Mantra — sacred words, or phrases that are repeated for the purposes of Self-realizing

Marma — a point on the skin, akin to an acupuncture point, manipulated during Ayurvedic massage and marma point therapies

Mauna — the practice of not speaking

Moksha — Self-realization; liberation

Paravac — the Supreme word

Paravak — the Supreme Goddess of the word

Pashyanti — Shakti manifesting as the desire of the Supreme Self to experience its own infinite potential

Prana — gross breath; subtle breath; subtle energy; air; vitality

Prarabdha karma — that portion of one's total karma that is ripe for expression in this lifetime

Prasad — a gift from God or Guru, often in the form of consecrated food

Pratyabhijña — Self-recognition, one of the major lineages comprising Kashmir Shaivism

Puja — ritual worship during which offerings are made to God or Guru

Sadhana — spiritual practice

Samskara — literally, "karmic scar"; a tendency comprised of karmic patterning

Sandhi — in between state; a gap; a juncture

Sangha — a spiritual community

Sannyasin — a renunciate

Satguru — root Guru; the teacher who shows you your real nature and guides you to Self-realization

Satya Yuga — the age of enlightenment lasting 1,728,000 years

Seva — service rendered to the Guru, Guru's family and spiritual community

Shakti — creative power; energy; the primordial female aspect of Reality; the power of Lord Shiva; the consort of Lord Shiva: the manifest world itself

Shiva — feeling-consciousness; the primordial male aspect of Reality; the consort of Shakti; the *adi*, or original Guru; awareness itself

Shunya — void; emptiness

Sushumna nadi — the central channel of the energy body

Tantrika — a Tantrik practitioner, or adept

Tapas — the practice of austerities

Trika — Kashmir Shaivism

Upaya — skillful means

Vaikhari — audible speech

Vairagya — detachment

Vidya Shakti — wisdom energy

Yoga — literally, "union"; a spiritual practice originating from the Tantrik Nath tradition of India and consisting of physical postures, mantra, breath control, internal ritual and visualization; all spiritual practices combined

Yogi/Yogini — a man or a woman who is adept at yoga

ALPHABETICAL INDEX OF TITLES

WORKS CITED

Abhinavagupta (Author), Jaideva Singh (Trans.), *A Trident of Wisdom: Translation of Paratrisika Vivarana*, SUNY Press, Albany, NY, 1988.

Abhinavagupta (Author), Boris Marjanovic (Trans.), *Abhinavagupta's Commentary on the Bhagavad Gita*, Rudra Press, Portland, Oregon, 2006.

Anandamayi Ma (Author), Atmananda (Trans.), *Matri Vani II*, Shree Shree Anandamayee Charitable Society, Varanasi, 1977.

Anandamayi Ma, "Sri Sri Ma's Utterances," *Ananda Varta*, Anandamayee Ma Sangha, Varanasi, Vol. 34.1, January 1987.

Anandamayi Ma (Author), Atmananda (Trans.), *Words of Sri Anandamayi Ma*, Shree Shree Anandamayee Sangha, Kankhal, India, 2008.

Dhar, Triloki Nath, *Saints and Sages of Kashmir*, APH Publishing, New Delhi, 2004.

Elliot, Mark (Director), *The Lion's Roar*, Festival Media, DVD, 2006.

Eugene, Simon (Director), *Love and the Art of Giving: 2007 Sat Chandi Maha Yajna*, DVD, 2007.

Jnanadeva (Author), B.P. Bahirat (Trans.), *Amritanubhava*, Popular Prakashan, Bombay, 1963.

Patten, Lesley Ann (Director), *Words of My Perfect Teacher*, ZIJI Film & Television, DVD, 2003.

Lakshmanjoo, Swami (Translation & commentary), *Vijnana Bhairava Tantra: The Practice of Centring Awareness*, Indica Books, Varanasi, 2002.

Lakshmanjoo, Swami (Translation & commentary) ; John Hughes (Ed.), *Shiva Sutras: The Supreme Awareness*, Universal Shaiva Fellowship, Culver City, CA, 2007.

Lalla (Author), Coleman Barks (Trans.), *Naked Song*, Maypop Books, Athens, Georgia, 1992. Used with permission of the publisher.

Lannoy, Richard, *Anandamayi Ma: Her Life and Wisdom*, Element, Rockport, MA, 1996. Video of Lannoy recounting the story of Ma and the young doctor: http://www.youtube.com/watch?v=47geMSDzf7Y.

Mackenzie, Vicki, *Cave in the Snow: Tenzin Palmo's Quest for Enlightenment*, Bloomsbury Paperbacks, New York, 1998.

Mukerji, Bithika, *A Bird on the Wing: Life and Teachings of Sri Ma Anandamayi*, Sri Satguru Publications, New Delhi, 1977.

Mukerji, Bithika, "Sri Ma Anandamayi," http://www.anandamayi.org/ashram/french/1i.htm, 1995, retrieved August 15, 2012.

Mt. Shasta, Peter, "A Trungpa Rincpoche Crazy Wisdom Teaching," *Elephant Journal, http://www.elephantjournal.com/2012/04/a-trungpa-rinpoche-crazy-wisdom-teaching--peter-mt-shasta/* , April 5, 2012, retrieved August 14, 2012.

Pynchon, Thomas, *Gravity's Rainbow*, Penguin Books, New York, 1995.

Rai, Ram Kumar, *Kularnava Tantra*, Prachya Prakashan, Varanasi, 1983.

Salzberg, Sharon, "Sit," *O Magazine, http://www.sharonsalzberg.com/archive/article/288,* November 1, 2002, retrieved on July 18, 2012.

Stevenson, Jayne (Director), *Yoga of the Heart: A Tantric Festival*, Big Shakti, DVD, 2006.

St. John of the Cross (Author), E. Allison Peers (Trans. & Ed.) *Dark Night of the Soul*, Doubleday, New York, 2005

Yogananda, Paramahansa, *Autobiography of a Yogi*, Self-Realization Fellowship, Los Angeles, 1988.

ABOUT JAYA KULA

Jaya Kula is a nonprofit spiritual organization in Portland, Oregon offering teachings in the traditions of direct realization Tantra (Kashmir Shaivism) and Anandamayi Ma. Shambhavi Sarasvati is the spiritual director.

Jaya Kula Press is owned and operated by Shambhavi Sarasvati in collaboration with generous students.

Mailing address:
4110 SE Hawthorne Blvd. #106
Portland, OR 97214

Email: shambhavi@jayakula.org
Phone: 503.902.1008
Website: jayakula.org

THANK YOU

Many thanks to Shaka McGlotten and Matridarshana Lamb for their wise and generous editorial assistance. Thanks also Richard and Dawn Plom for helping to provide the iPad on which I was able to complete much of the editing of this book while in India. Finally, heartfelt thanks to my students and the larger Jaya Kula community whose sincere efforts to wake up and the questions they have asked along the way informed much of the writing offered here.

JAYA KULA PRESS TITLES
by SHAMBHAVI SARASVATI

Pilgrims to Openness:
Direct Realization Tantra in Everyday Life, 2009

Tantra: the Play of Awakening, 2012

Made in the USA
Middletown, DE
16 February 2017